Praise for *Teach Happier This School Year:*
40 Weeks of Inspiration and Reflection

The greatest advantage we can cultivate in the modern world is a positive and connected brain. And the better we get at research, the more we are learning how seemingly small changes to our mindset or behavior make massive and quantifiable impacts not only to our own mindset and outcomes, but to the entire ecosystem around us at home, work, or school. We can now measure a ripple effect to people three or four degrees from the original positive habit, which means our actions and mindset impact people we never even meet. Suzanne Dailey, a champion of this positive research, shows you clearly and practically how to make a daily practice of shifting our mindset and our culture to raise well-being, connection, and purpose.

—Shawn Achor, *New York Times* bestselling author of
Big Potential and *The Happiness Advantage*

More than ever, we as educators need a book that lifts our spirits and fills our hearts with joy, while at the same time giving us realistic, job-embedded ideas to try at work each day. *Teach Happier This School Year* is that book. Suzanne Dailey has masterfully woven together two decades of experience in the classroom with her passion for positive psychology and helping others. Through sharing stories that everyone in education can relate to, she invites us to make small shifts in our thinking, words, and actions that will help us to find more happiness in both our professional and our personal lives. Make yourself a priority this year and join the Teach Happier community!

—Rob Dunlop, author of
STRIVE for Happiness in Education

If Suzanne Dailey is writing a book, I can tell you it's moving to the top of my reading list! *Teach Happier This School Year* has brought me so much joy as I explored the small shifts that infuse joy into our lives at school and at home. There has never been a timelier topic for educators to commit themselves to. Whether you are looking for a quick read or a deep dive to influence a huge life shift, this book is perfect for you to begin taking actionable steps toward success.

—Rae Hughart, Teach Better Team

Teach Happier This School Year comes along at just the right time to get us back on track when it comes to our personal well-being. This reflective journal is filled with practical stories, anecdotes, tools, and minilessons that will challenge you to make small but powerful shifts in your thinking and behavior throughout the school year and highlight your happiest moments.

—Jimmy Casas, leadership coach, educator, author, and speaker

Teach Happier This School Year is the book I didn't even know I needed in my life. Happiness is such an important part of our lives, yet it so often takes a back seat to other things we have going on. Suzanne does an amazing job not just writing about being happy, but providing tools, resources, and actionable ways for educators to find that happiness. Happiness isn't one more thing you need to work on—it is *the* thing we need to be focusing on. I just love how Suzanne tells stories, provides quotes from educators and leaders around the world, and lays it out where, for me, there is absolutely nothing to refute about what we should all be doing.

—Adam Welcome, educator, author, speaker, and podcaster

TEACH HAPPIER THIS SCHOOL YEAR

TEACH

40 WEEKS
of Inspiration
and Reflection

HAPPIER

THIS

SCHOOL YEAR

SUZANNE DAILEY

 ascd | Arlington, Virginia USA

2800 Shirlington Road, Suite 1001 • Arlington, VA 22206 USA
Phone: 800-933-2723 or 703-578-9600 • Fax: 703-575-5400
Website: www.ascd.org • Email: member@ascd.org
Author guidelines: www.ascd.org/write

Penny Reinart, *Deputy Executive Director;* Genny Ostertag, *Managing Director, Book Acquisitions & Editing;* Susan Hills, *Senior Acquisitions Editor;* Mary Beth Nielsen, *Director, Book Editing;* Miriam Calderone, *Editor;* Thomas Lytle, *Creative Director;* Donald Ely, *Art Director;* Lisa Hill, *Graphic Designer;* Cynthia Stock, *Typesetter;* Kelly Marshall, *Production Manager;* Shajuan Martin, *E-Publishing Specialist*

All web links in this book are correct as of the publication date below but may have become inactive or otherwise modified since that time. If you notice a deactivated or changed link, please email books@ascd.org with the words "Link Update" in the subject line. In your message, please specify the web link, the book title, and the page number on which the link appears.

PAPERBACK ISBN: 978-1-4166-3166-8   ASCD product #123027   n1/23

PDF E-BOOK ISBN: 978-1-4166-3167-5; see Books in Print for other formats.

Quantity discounts are available: email programteam@ascd.org or call 800-933-2723, ext. 5773, or 703-575-5773. For desk copies, go to www.ascd.org/deskcopy.

Library of Congress Cataloging-in-Publication Data

Names: Dailey, Suzanne, author.
Title: Teach happier this school year : 40 weeks of inspiration and
    reflection / Suzanne Dailey.
Description: Arlington, VA : ASCD, [2023] | Includes bibliographical
    references and index.
Identifiers: LCCN 2022037522 (print) | LCCN 2022037523 (ebook) | ISBN
    9781416631668 (paperback) | ISBN 9781416631675 (pdf)
Subjects: LCSH: Teaching. | Teachers.
Classification: LCC LB1025.3 .D337 2023 (print) | LCC LB1025.3 (ebook) |
    DDC 371.102—dc23/eng/20221019
LC record available at https://lccn.loc.gov/2022037522
LC ebook record available at https://lccn.loc.gov/2022037523

31 30 29 28 27 26 25 24 23   2 3 4 5 6 7 8 9 10 11 12

To Beverly Elaine and Emerson Elaine:
my two favorite teachers.

Teach Happier This School Year: 40 Weeks of Inspiration and Reflection

Welcome to the Teach Happier Community!

Congratulations! You are beginning the journey to prioritize your well-being and happiness this upcoming school year! For 5–10 minutes every week, from about early September to late June, you are going to learn how to make small shifts that, when practiced over time, will help you feel more balanced, content, and aligned.

Spoiler alert: In this book you won't hear about quick fixes like 10-minute massage chairs or bubble baths. Although lovely, these things won't bring long-term happiness. And here's another spoiler: Happiness is a *discipline*. I know, right? Seems to take the fun out of it. But think about it: If you want to become a better runner, you run more; if you want to become a better cook, you invest more time in the kitchen. In the same way, if you want to get happier and live a more content, aligned life, you must invest time in learning how to do so—and then be disciplined about applying this new learning to your life.

Let's be honest: We are all busy educators and don't have time for a grand, sweeping 180-degree turn—but we *can* envision and act upon a series of smaller 2-degree shifts. Think about a plane that gradually turns 2 degrees every few minutes. That plane will end up in a very different location from where it was originally headed!

If you think about happiness as a *discipline* and an *investment*, you can understand that the smallest shifts are what bring the biggest gifts over time. When you become disciplined about applying those 2-degree shifts, you will see and feel positive change in your life. What's more, you may find some of these shifts surprisingly easy to make. The goal is not to overwhelm by urging you to make great changes but, rather, to help streamline your energies toward incrementally adjusting your thoughts, language, and actions in ways that will gradually increase your overall happiness. Some of these strategies are based on common wisdom, but they may not all be common practice—yet.

My inspiration for this reflective journal comes from various experiences I've had throughout my 22 years as an educator. Currently, I am an instructional coach for the Central Bucks School District, the third-largest school district in Pennsylvania. I have the honor of working alongside 650 of the greatest elementary teachers on the planet. I'm in up to 15 different classrooms in any given week teaching, consulting, troubleshooting, or planning. I'm also supporting, loving, celebrating, counseling, and listening. Prior to coaching, I was a 4th grade teacher and a reading specialist for primary and intermediate students.

Another source of inspiration has come from the research I've done during the last 15 years. For instance, did you know about the "happiness curve" we tend to follow as we age? A well-documented longitudinal study asked people about their levels of happiness at different points in their life and found that, on average, childhood innocence and joy fades around age 20, and then there is a stunning decline in happiness until age 50, when it rises again (*The Economist*, 2010). Fifty! That's 30 years of trying to figure out how to meet the demands of work, family, and aging as we wait for happiness to climb again.

It can be a discouraging journey, but some of the strategies in this book may help you navigate these times as a rational optimist (more on this later).

Our work as educators is so human. We are literally in the business of *people!* My interactions in education combined with my voracious reading, listening, and research into positive psychology, social science, and neuroscience allow me to share what research tells us and blend those insights with practical ideas for both school and home.

Our goal as educators is to be present and effective for the students in front of us, the colleagues beside us, and the families within our homes. But we can accomplish this only if we take some time to focus on ourselves and invest time to nurture our own happiness. We can't just wait for the universe to magically make this happen; we have to get disciplined and do the work ourselves. Simply put, it's an inside job. This reflective journal will help you to frame this work and better organize your happiness journey.

Please know that when the word *happiness* is referenced, it doesn't mean "good vibes only" or "tra-la-la-ing" through all the hard stuff. It means feeling content, aligned, and balanced in a world that often feels scary, off-kilter, and unpredictable. It's important for you to know that I am not writing this book in a meadow of sunshine and rainbows. Although I have a pretty high happiness baseline, I am writing this book during the hardest and saddest years of my life. In the past year, I lost my beloved mom at 67 years old to Alzheimer's, I lost a best friend to a brain tumor, another close friend was diagnosed with ALS, and I am navigating how to best support our neurodiverse child. This year has been challenging, exhausting, worrisome, and heartbreaking. I share this with you because I want you to know that every strategy in this book has been put to the test during great days, average days, and days that left me speechless and in tears. I have walked the talk in real time, in real life, and I'm hopeful my reflections on these challenging times can benefit you.

And that's just personally. Professionally, I continue to help colleagues navigate this postpandemic "new normal" as we discern what to hang on to and what to let go of moving forward. We are working to address learning gaps, social-emotional needs, and relationships with community members while tirelessly trying to stay anchored in teaching and learning.

The reading, listening, researching, and practicing I have been doing for the past 15 years gave me the tools to help move through the most challenging season of my life. Regardless of where you are right now, these strategies, when practiced over time, have the potential to make a positive impact on your life, both personally and professionally.

Although this book is written to give you practical ideas as you make small shifts in thoughts, language, and actions, it is not intended to cure issues such as racial injustice, underfunded schools, or the heartbreaking grief of student loss. Although we cannot fix the global systems and structures that often dictate our work's challenges, we *can* adjust the systems and structures of our *individual* lives, one 2-degree shift at a time! Once we better understand ourselves, we can be in a better space to contribute to our classrooms, our homes, and the world.

Thank you for being open to a year of gentle growth for yourself as a professional and as a *person*. We all play many roles above and beyond our role as educators. We are parents, partners, siblings, daughters/sons, aunts/uncles, and friends. If we want to be healthier versions of ourselves in all these roles, we have to be open to the idea that we can learn and grow from the findings in neuroscience and in positive and social psychology. As my favorite author, Kelly Corrigan, says on her podcast *Kelly Corrigan Wonders,* "We are in our heads all of the time. We might as well make it nice up there."

"Joy is the oxygen for doing hard things."

—Gary Haugen

How to Use This Journal

You will notice this reflective journal extends over 40 weeks. These weeks are organized into four "marking periods" to mimic a typical school calendar and honor the natural feelings we experience as educators at different points of the school year. In each 10-week "marking period," you will do the following:

- Read the designated chapter connecting real life with positive psychology. I recommend doing this on Sunday afternoons or evenings, as the "Sunday Scaries" start creeping in. Not only will these chapters help those Sunday Scaries, but reading them will ensure you start your week in the healthiest headspace and heartspace, as realistically as possible.

- Incorporate a small shift in your upcoming week and create one personalized goal.

- At the end of the week, reflect on how that small shift has increased your happiness at work and/or at home.

- Celebrate your week with a "Weekly Win." This is where you "scan for the good" and write down the happiest personal or professional moment of your week. (By the time you are finished with this school year, you will have an inspiring collection of at least 40 joyful moments from the year!)

- If you see the Teach Happier Lesson logo, that means there is an accompanying 10- to 15-minute minilesson you can use to share your new learning with students! Colleagues and I have taught these lessons with real students in real time and have found them to make a positive impact in classroom culture and community. If you like these lessons, new ones are uploaded frequently at www.suzannedailey.com/lessons.

Just as you do for your students, you will take a moment to reflect on your personal growth with a report card at the end of each marking period. You will have the time and space to review the main takeaways of each of the 10 chapters shared throughout the marking period and reflect on how the small shifts you've taken have positively impacted you at work and at home. This is also an opportunity to consider creating space for any of the small shifts you didn't have the bandwidth for earlier; the included prompts will help you do this with ease.

Before You Begin Week 1

Here you are at the beginning of a new school year. You're rested, energized, and as optimistic as you'll be all year long. This is a good time to take inventory and set some intentions for the upcoming year so you can learn from your past and think of your future. Start by making this pledge:

> As a rational optimist, I will know what I can incorporate in my personal and professional life to feel as content, aligned, and balanced as realistically possible.

Then, consider this essential question:

> What practices based in positive psychology will make a positive impact in my life, personally and professionally?

To help put this pledge and essential question into context, shift your focus toward someone at work whom you would describe as happy (not *annoyingly* happy, just regular makes-you-smile-and-feel-good happy). Now that you have that person in mind, extend your thinking and consider their productivity, creativity, and energy. What do you notice? According to Rob Dunlop (2020), research shows that happy people are 37 percent more productive and 23 percent more energetic than their peers, and they have *three times* the amount of creativity. I can't imagine anyone wants *less* of these qualities. By reflecting on your current patterns of language, thoughts, and actions, you can make subtle shifts that increase your baseline levels of happiness—and in the process, become more productive, energetic, and creative.

John Dewey once said, "We do not learn from experience . . . we learn from *reflecting* on experience." Many of us believe that no experience, good or bad, is ever wasted, since they all help us learn and grow. So before getting started on the work of this journal, take some time to engage in the following reflection exercises, which include probing questions inspired by Emily P. Freeman's work (2019). Though I've provided some examples to get you started, this is a space for you to personalize the path of your upcoming journey. You will notice that my examples in the first two reflection boxes include actions within my realm of influence and control; I encourage you, too, to use examples that are within your own realm of influence and control so you can feel anchored as you move throughout the next 40 weeks.

Life at Home and School

Thinking about the past school year, fill in Reflection Boxes 1 and 2.

Reflection Box 1

What Worked (Professionally)	What Didn't Work (Professionally)
Ex.: Sticking to clear boundaries at nighttime to decrease my availability to colleagues (texts, emails) and increase my availability to family	Ex.: During big projects, not accepting help from colleagues when it was offered (in other words, trying to do everything myself)
What Worked (Personally)	**What Didn't Work (Personally)**
Ex.: Working with Pat to allocate kid and house tasks so our limited energies could be put toward the right things	Ex.: Hanging on to traditions/expectations that left me tired and frustrated because that's what "has always been"

Reflection Box 2

What Was Life GIVING? (Professionally)	What Was Life DRAINING? (Professionally)
Ex.: Collaborating with new colleagues to create resources for fellow educators both in and out of our district, like the Happiness Advent Calendar with Rob Dunlop	*Ex.: Helping colleagues adjust and readjust to changing health and safety plans and encouraging them to remain focused on the most important work*

What Was Life GIVING? (Personally)	What Was Life DRAINING? (Personally)
Ex.: Prioritizing time and space to be with those who make me feel good	*Ex.: Saying yes to people or events when I knew it wouldn't add to my or my family's overall wellness during sad/stressful seasons*

What Is Something Positive I Want to Acknowledge or Remember?	What Is Something Negative I Want to Acknowledge or Remember?
Ex.: How friends and family showed up (literally and metaphorically!) when I needed them the most	*Ex.: Falling short and not showing up for friends or family when they needed me because I didn't have the necessary bandwidth or capacity to do so*

Next, fast-forward to thinking about the last day of school and complete Reflection Box 3.

Reflection Box 3

How do YOU want to feel at the end of the year?	
How do you want your STUDENTS to feel at the end of the year?	
How do you want your COLLEAGUES to feel at the end of the year?	
How do you want your FAMILY to feel at the end of the year?	

Relationships

Complete Reflection Box 4.

Reflection Box 4

Relationships I've Nurtured in the Past Year	Relationships I Want to Nurture This School Year

Your Happiness Baseline

Now, reflect on the happiness continuum, inspired by the work of Mark Koester (2018), shown in Figure i.1. Where do you fall on this scale?

Figure i.1. Happiness Continuum

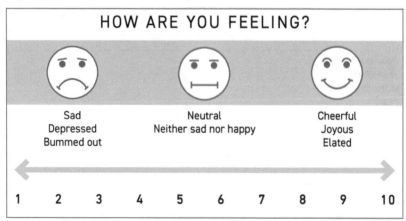

Think about your number on the happiness continuum and, in the following space, jot down a few reasons *why* you feel the way you feel. Knowing where you are on this continuum is one part of understanding where you are now and where you want these 2-degree shifts to take you. The more important part is recognizing *why* you may be feeling this way. This can help clarify which shifts may make a greater impact in your life at school or at home.

What's the Story You Want to Tell This Year?

Let's begin with the end in mind. As you embark on this school year, consider the headspace you, your colleagues, your students, and your family want to be in. Knowing your final destination will help prioritize the 2-degree shifts in thoughts, language, and actions to get you there!

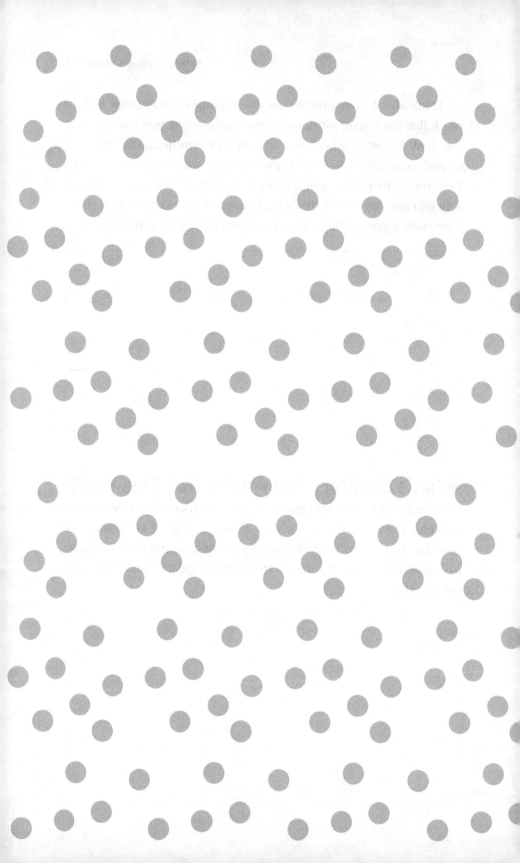

"Don't just start
your school year.
Begin your legacy."

— Wendy Hankins (@MrsHankinsClass) —

1

Your Legacy Begins This Week

Well, here you are. Gearing up for the first week of school. Your optimism is soaring and you feel recharged from the summer. At this point, most of us are looking forward to getting back into the routine of school and connecting with colleagues and students.

We all got into teaching for different reasons. I am a teacher because of my 4th grade teacher. Ms. Nelson was the kind of educator who had really high expectations but also showed her students how much she loved them. I'd do anything she asked me to do—I knew she would push me while supporting me every step of the way.

Fast-forward 14 years to the open house before my first official day of teaching 4th grade. This is the day students and parents come in to check out their classroom and meet their teacher before the year officially begins. As Miss Olney, I welcomed parents and students into the classroom, feeling underprepared for and over-whelmed by the responsibility I was about to assume at the young age of 22. Nevertheless, I tried my best to play the role of an adult in my Steve Madden shoes and outfit from The Limited. A constant stream of new students and their parents (who seemed *so old* to me at the time!) came through asking questions, finding lockers, and dropping off fresh new folders, pencils, and crayons. There was so much to take in during this busy time. My teachermind and teacher-heart were racing!

And then time stopped. There she was. I'd recognize that beautiful white hair anywhere. There was Ms. Nelson, my former 4th grade teacher, standing in the doorway of *my* 4th grade classroom. I walked away from a parent asking about field trips to the Erie Canal and went right over to the person who had inspired me to teach. We hugged, we cried, and she wished me a wonderful year ahead, leaving me a glass apple for my desk. It was the ultimate full-circle experience.

I firmly believe there are no mistakes on class rosters. Each and every adult and student in your classroom is there to teach others something. As you prepare to launch a new school year, you will undoubtedly become someone else's Ms. Nelson. And it's not just our hearts that tell us this is true: Research proves that the greatest factor in students' success is the quality of their teachers and the relationships they build with them (Hattie, 2012). In 20, 30, or 50 years, a student will think of you and say your name. How will you want to be remembered?

That glass apple has followed me to every classroom since that day. When I look at it, it reminds me of the opportunities I have each day to make a positive impact on the lives of kids. Ms. Nelson left a legacy that literally shaped my future.

As a postscript to this full-circle moment, while I was putting the final touches on this book, a former 4th grade student of mine, Julia, reached out to share the news that *she* was just hired to be a 4th grade teacher—*in our school district.* Where I get to *coach and work alongside our new teachers as they begin their professional career!* It's bananas, and what I know for sure is that it doesn't get any better than this.

You have a Ms. Nelson. You have a Julia. Anchoring ourselves to this truth is how we recapture our purpose and rediscover our joy in this essential work.

If you're breathing, somebody needs your gifts.

Your legacy begins this week.

Small Shifts, Big Gifts

TEACH HAPPIER

Fast-forward to the end of your school year. How do you want your students to feel about their year? Think of *one* thing you can do or say to create a classroom culture that will accomplish that.

Set a personal or professional goal for the week based on one small shift.

Weekly Win: At the end of the week, jot down one great thing that happened.

2

You Will Be Remembered for the Way You Love

I wrote this chapter during one of the hardest years of my life: 2021, when I lost my beloved mom to Alzheimer's at just 67 years old. She was my person. We always just "got" each other. The greatest honor of my lifetime is being Beverly's daughter, and losing her is the loss of my lifetime.

My mom passed in June, and all I can really remember from that summer is that I spent it grieving in big and little ways, because her departure broke me. Those initial weeks learning how to move through my days without her was one of the most tender, exhausting seasons I've ever experienced. Then, before I knew it, I had to muster up the energy and optimism to begin a whole new school year and motivate others to do the same. This felt nearly impossible at times. I was able to find some perspective by looking back to the eulogy I'd written and delivered. This sacred piece of writing wasn't difficult to prepare, because my mom is easy to talk about and celebrate. She loved lots of people and loved them well. Reflecting on the theme of her eulogy may help to anchor you and provide some much-needed perspective as you enter this new school year: *We will be remembered for the way we love.*

One more time for those in the back: *We will be remembered for the way we love.*

I often work with new teachers, helping acclimate them to the district and its high expectations. One time, I was working with a new teacher whose questions all had to do with logistics: "When do I practice for the fire drill? Where are the hall passes? When am I getting observed?" Although completely realistic and necessary, her questions left out one important thing: her *students*. Please know that I answered her questions, but I also folded in some questions of my own: "Do your students seem comfortable in the classroom? What has been successful as you helped build classroom community in these past two weeks? Have parents shared any celebrations or concerns? How do you begin and end your day with your students?"

You may be getting a little task-focused as you settle into the routines of Week 2, but right now you're also as rested and optimistic as you'll be all year. This is a good time to reflect on how you are going to *love* this year—since, ultimately, it is your love that students will remember most.

Loving Your Students

What conditions do you want to cultivate this year so your students bloom spectacularly? Fast-forward to the last day of school and consider how you want your students to feel. Are they leaving the year feeling supported, important, and loved? Now rewind and envision the small moves in language and actions you can take to accomplish that. How will you be remembered by your students this coming June?

Loving Your Colleagues

Our colleagues directly influence our overall happiness. We spend so much time together! What actions within your realm of influence or control support mutually supportive and beneficial relationships with those you work closest with? How will your collegial relationships become stronger this school year?

Loving Your Family

During the COVID-19 pandemic, many of us reprioritized our time and began to set healthier boundaries, including protecting quality time with family. This year, be sure to do what you can to ensure that you love and care for your students at school while also conserving enough energy to love and care for your family, whether they live with you or elsewhere. How do you want your home team, your family, to feel when you cross the finish line of this school year?

Loving Yourself

It is necessary to care for yourself before you can care for others. How will you give yourself permission to nurture *you*? (Dedicating a few minutes each week to this reflective journal is one way!) What professional and personal boundaries do you plan to set *and honor* in this upcoming school year?

Bob Goff, author of *Undistracted* (2022), says it perfectly: "We will be known for our opinions but remembered for the love we gave to everyone around us . . . the clarity of purpose, undistracted energy, selfless love, and unselfish pursuits you bring into the world will be your legacy. Everything else will look like a distraction by comparison" (p. 21).

Your invitation for reflection this week is inspired by my mom and comes directly from the conclusion of her eulogy:

> Here's to quietly tucking tiny moments of love into our days.
> Here's to our eyes sparkling when we see someone we love.
> Here's to living a life grounded in gratitude and abundance as
>   love's boots on the ground.
> Here's to being remembered for the way we love.

Small Shifts, Big Gifts

Revisit Reflection Box 4 on page 6. Are there any relationships you want to add? What relationships can you strengthen in the upcoming week? Also, glance back at the short sentences in the previous section about how you want your family, colleagues, students, and self to feel at the end of the school year. You may find you want to revise those entries a bit, or you may be encouraged to focus on someone specifically to love and nurture.

Set a personal or professional goal for the week based on one small shift.

Weekly Win: At the end of the week, jot down one great thing that happened.

3

Work/Life Satisfaction

Throughout the next 38 weeks, you will learn a lot—and you will also *unlearn* a lot. This week you will explore one of the most important things you'll need to unlearn: the very concept of work/life balance.

Have you ever Googled something like, "How can I achieve work/life balance" or "Strategies to help balance work and home"? If you have, you more than likely got a bunch of nonscientific articles or Pinterest-perfect quotes that left you feeling less than satisfied. There's a good reason for that: There is actually *no such thing* as work/life balance.

Nope. I'm sorry to break it to you, but it simply doesn't exist. Which is why nobody can attain it!

"By its very definition," writes Staci Thetford (2018), "balance is spending equal parts of your time between work and all of your non-work-related demands." It's a lovely definition, and an even lovelier sentiment. But when you stop to think about it, have you ever had a truly 50/50 split between work and home? I sure haven't. Find me in September getting the school year started, and I'm probably 75 percent work and 25 percent home. The week before winter break? I'm lucky if I'm 20 percent work and 80 percent home. Parent conference week? Back up to 75 percent at work (you should see the dinners my family eats during this time!). If there is a family emergency or great need at home, I'll be 85 percent focused there and trying to muster up the other 15 percent for work. And over time I have learned that these fluctuations are perfectly reasonable and healthy to accept.

It's not that I am doing life "wrong"; rather, I am putting my energies toward what's needed at the time.

Have I ever truly been 50/50? Not a chance. I am never killing it at work *and* killing it at home. And that's OK! It's OK because it depends on the season and needs at home and at work. Part of the reason it gets so frustrating when we feel unbalanced is because we've been given the narrative that work/life balance is realistically attainable. I would like to invite you to consider a small shift in language: It's not work/life balance you're looking for. It's work/life *satisfaction*.

Say it again: *work/life satisfaction.*

Can you be balanced in both places simultaneously? Nope.

Can you be *satisfied* in both places simultaneously? Yep. *This* is attainable.

So instead of beating yourself up because you don't feel completely aligned and balanced between work and home, revise your thoughts and language. Understand that the infamous work/life balance is simply not attainable. What *is* attainable—and sustainable—is achieving a level of satisfaction in both places as you move through your days.

Small Shifts, Big Gifts

See if the small shift in language from *work/life balance* to *work/life satisfaction* helps you create realistic, manageable expectations for your personal and professional life.

Set a personal or professional goal for the week based on one small shift.

Weekly Win: At the end of the week, jot down one great thing that happened.

4

Rational Optimism

The term *toxic positivity* has gotten a lot of attention over the past couple of years. It was a fascinating concept to me (and one we'll investigate later in this book) because I didn't realize there could be such a thing as being *too* positive. But it turns out that we can all exude toxic positivity when we don't allow someone who is struggling to feel that it's OK to struggle and honor those feelings.

This book does not have many rules, but here is one of them: There is no room for toxic positivity in this Teach Happier space—but there is plenty of room for *rational optimism.*

Here's a million-dollar question: If you saw a cup, and half of it contained water, how would you describe that cup? Half-full? Half-empty? What if I told you it was neither—it was *refillable?*

Seeing the cup as refillable is the mark of a *rational optimist.*

Brian Clark (2019) defines rational optimism as "taking a realistic assessment of the present moment. It means maintaining the belief that you can put one foot in front of the other, take action, and overcome a challenge or reach a goal" (para. 3). In other words, a rational optimist understands that some parts of our lives are fixed and out of our control—things like genetics, our relatives, the weather, the current political climate, or certain health diagnoses.

Positive psychologists will tell us that these fixed elements make up about 10 to 20 percent of our lives. And that's great news, because it means that we *can* influence 80 to 90 percent of our lives! Even in the middle of really hard seasons, we still control how we perceive and respond to the world. That is the definition of rational optimism: It's the understanding that, though a few things may be out of our control, those few things are *finite,* and we can still influence most of our lives.

Do you remember those first tense weeks of the pandemic? The news reports, school closings, predictions, and theories were so frightening and uncertain, and everything felt like it was out of our control. "While we have minimal control over the events that befall us," writes Frank Bruni, "we have the final say over how we regard and react to them" (2022, p. 86).

On March 29, 2020, actor John Krasinski showed us rational optimism in action with his YouTube show *Some Good News.* He began all nine episodes the same way—by acknowledging this was a scary, uncertain time—but then spent the rest of the show highlighting good news: a community coming together to donate food to those who needed it, families helping animals in need, teachers reading to students in driveways. It was his way of saying, "Hey, world, this is hard. But we can do hard things and we can do good things together." Good ol' Jim Halpert from television's *The Office* is a model of rational optimism.

Krasinski's show inspired guidance counselor Jenn Horan at Titus Elementary School in Warrington, Pennsylvania, to create her own version for the school community, *Let's Hear It for the Joy!* (A nod to Deniece Williams's 1984 hit "Let's Hear It for the Boy"—and I apologize for getting that gem stuck in your head this week.) Jenn began her weekly video broadcast by telling the 644 students at Titus Elementary that adults from school missed them all very much, and this was a difficult time for grown-ups, kids, and families. After that, Jenn highlighted how the local community was donating goods to those in need, how some Titus parents who were health-care workers continued to help others, and how some families were helping each other out like they never had before. Rational optimism at its finest.

I cannot control or fix my buddy Bryan's heartbreaking ALS diagnosis. But I can certainly impact the way I show up for his family. I cannot control or fix the struggles our neurodiverse child experiences. But I can influence the supports that are put into place at home and at school. And losing my mom? The very worst thing that has ever happened to me? Although I can't bring her back, I get to decide how to carry on her legacy every single day. I acknowledge what's really hard and fixed, but I understand I can still impact that fixed situation with rational optimism.

As you enter the week ahead, acknowledge both what may be difficult in your life *and* what you can influence positively. Life is hard *and* beautiful. Navigating your life as a rational optimist allows you to see both sides and do the next right thing in a healthy way, in both your personal and professional lives.

Remember: Your cup is refillable. As a rational optimist, think about what's within your control and use that to positively impact your life.

TEACH HAPPIER

Small Shifts, Big Gifts

Make a list of things that are out of your control both at work and at home, then list what is *within* your realm of control. This can help you get closer to becoming a rational optimist and putting energy toward the things that fill your cup personally and professionally.

Set a personal or professional goal for the week based on one small shift.

Weekly Win: At the end of the week, jot down one great thing that happened.

5

Happiness Is a Discipline

"Suzanne, how are you so happy?"

I get asked this question often—like, maybe three times a week. Well, dear reader, let me pull back the curtain and let you in on a little secret: I'm not happy all the time—that's just not realistic. But I do believe I experience happiness and joy more often than most, and that's because I treat it like a discipline.

A discipline? For *happiness?*

Kind of takes the fun right out of it, right?

Actually, it should seem logical. If I want to be an overall happier person, I need to treat happiness like any other skill and practice it. As you read and work through this book, you will see that the smallest shifts, practiced over time consistently, bring significant, positive energy into our lives.

There are some natural times in the school year when we need to be more disciplined about our own happiness and being in control of our morale—and now is one of those times. During these first few weeks of establishing routines, enforcing expectations, and getting to know your students, taking care of your own sanity may fall toward the bottom of your never-ending list of tasks.

So let's get disciplined about prioritizing our happiness! As James Clear (2019) suggests, it's not what we do every once in a while with intensity that makes the difference—it's what we do *consistently* that does. "Most people need consistency more than they need intensity," he writes (para. 8). "Intensity makes a good story. Consistency makes progress" (para. 11).

In an effort to put this idea of happiness as a discipline into practice, I'd like to invite you to do something that my dear friend Melissa Brevic does with 6th grade students and that I have done with thousands of students and adults during workshop sessions:

- Start by asking yourself: "What makes me happy?"

- Next, grab an index card or any piece of paper and jot down 10 things that make you happy. (My list includes my family, reading, writing, catching up with friends, running, nature, music, laughter, traveling, and animals.)

- Pick *one* of the things on your list that genuinely adds to your overall happiness—your contentment, alignment, and balance. For me, it's reading at night. Reading helps quiet my mind, put the day behind, and get into someone else's story. It also helps tire my eyes so I can fall asleep!

- Now this is where it can get fun and artsy. Shape a pipe cleaner so it represents that one thing. Some examples of what people have made in workshops include representations of their pet, nature, music, or reading. Don't have a pipe cleaner? No problem—just draw a picture of what makes you happy on a piece of paper.

- Finally, put this pipe cleaner or drawing somewhere you look often (my pipe cleaner shaped like a book hangs on the corner of my bathroom mirror so I see it multiple times a day). Seeing it will overtly remind you to make the time and space to do this thing. It's a way to proactively protect your happiness.

When things get overwhelming, logistically or emotionally, I can find myself thinking, "I'll just finish that before I go to bed," and skipping nighttime reading. But those 15 minutes of reading bring me more peace, quiet, and restoration than any other 15 minutes of my day. Therefore, I have to be disciplined and protect this activity. Fiercely. Seeing my little pipe cleaner book in the mirror multiple times of day encourages me to *make* the time for the things that contribute to my peace and happiness. It's just another small, short-term shift that will bring immeasurable gifts in the long run.

Treating happiness as a discipline has been one of the most impactful 2-degree shifts I have made in my thoughts and actions. It helps me understand what I need to prioritize in an effort to protect and preserve my head and heart. So when I'm asked, "Suzanne, how can you be so happy this time of the school year?" I respond, "Especially at a time like this, how can I *not* be? Our joy has never been needed more!"

At this busy time of our school year, make your happiness a priority and protect it fiercely. Right now in the world, so much is out of your control, yet you have tremendous influence on your happiness within your smaller world.

Get disciplined about it—and get happy!

TEACH
HAPPIER

Small Shifts, Big Gifts

Follow the steps on page 27. Check in with yourself throughout the week and see how it makes you feel when you consciously and consistently create time and space for the things that help you feel content, aligned, and balanced.

Set a personal or professional goal for the week based on one small shift.

Weekly Win: At the end of the week, jot down one great thing that happened.

Objective: Students will be able to prioritize what makes them happy and plan time and space for those activities.

Procedure

1. Explain to students how happiness is a discipline and how we can impact or influence how happy our lives are.

2. Model your top-10 list of things that make you happy and have students create one of their own.

3. Model choosing one thing from your list and creating a pipe cleaner object. Students will then do the same.

4. Explain that you will find a place to hang your pipe cleaner where you will see it often, and encourage students to do the same.

5. Later, have follow-up conversations about the positive impact making time and space for this activity has created in your life and your students' lives.

The Importance of *You*

The other day I was driving to school listening to one of my favorite podcasts, *Kelly Corrigan Wonders*. Corrigan's (2021) fierce wondering in this episode was, *What contributes to our happiness?* She highlighted a study from M. Scott Peck's *The Road Less Traveled* (2012) that is important to learn about at the beginning of your Teach Happier journey. As Corrigan tells it, the individuals conducting the study took the top 12 performing members in each branch of the military—those who had won awards, maintained healthy social relationships, were well respected by peers, and felt highly confident and aligned—and asked them, "What is the most important thing in your life?"

Wow. That's quite a question. As I was driving, I felt confident that I had an idea of some of the answers, and I am sure you do, too. I was ready for things like faith, family, God, sense of purpose, and so on.

As it happens, every single person had the same answer, and it wasn't any of the things just mentioned. The most important thing in their lives, they said, was *themselves*.

While this may seem weird at first, it really makes perfect sense. Essentially, the respondents were saying that they understood they themselves had the biggest influence on their lives. The choices they made, both big and small, helped determine how happy and successful they would ultimately be. The respondents went on to say that their relationships were healthy because they weren't relying on their partner, children, friends, or colleagues to make them happier. They knew that was up to *them*.

This is such an important lesson. Sometimes I want to blame my colleague, district, state mandate, or spouse or relative for some frustrating aspect of my day and make them magically fix the situation so I can instantly feel better. But we can't rely on those around us to determine our happiness; that work belongs to us. It can sometimes be *hard* work, but once we better understand those small shifts that are within our realm of control, we can take our happiness into our own hands.

So look around your life and examine your thoughts, actions, and language. What do you think, do, or say that negatively impacts your happiness? Conversely, what do you think, do, or say that *positively* impacts your happiness? This little inventory will help anchor you as you continue to learn more about the science of happiness and how it can benefit you at school and at home.

TEACH HAPPIER

Small Shifts, Big Gifts

Think about the study from Peck's book as you move through your week. Examine your life to see if you tend to rely on others to increase your happiness at work or at home. If you notice this happening, consider what is within your realm of control when discerning your next right thing.

Set a personal or professional goal for the week based on one small shift.

Weekly Win: At the end of the week, jot down one great thing that happened.

7

Sideline Conversations

I was at my son's basketball game when I overheard one mom politely asking another mom, "How did the year go for Shane? Is he excited for summer?"

"This year? This year was unlike any other," Shane's mother replied.

Oh boy, I thought. Here we go. This could be good. This could be bad.

Reader, it was beautiful.

"The year started really rocky," continued Shane's mom. "You heard me talking in October about Shane's struggles. Lots of people were telling me lots of things about him with all kinds of numbers and percentages and using words like *time on task, attention, impulsivity*. I could hardly keep up with it all."

"Oh, I'm so sorry," said the other mom.

"Oh, don't be sorry. We had Ms. Cobble. She *got* Shane. Like, she *really* got him. I honestly don't know exactly what she did, but I do know she worked with him and tried all kinds of things all year long until things clicked with Shane. And get this: We had a meeting last week, and every single one of those data points and percentages was so much better than it was at the beginning of the year—*literally every single one!* He feels better, I feel better, we all feel so much better. Ms. Cobble was like magic for my boy."

As George Couros (2018) says, "Teachers are trajectory changers."

Ms. Cobble literally changed the trajectory for this 9-year-old, and his path will forever be different because of her.

The takeaway from this eavesdropped conversation? Just as we often plan backward for units and lessons, it's important to plan backward for the school year.

In these first few weeks of school, let this story from last spring fuel the fall and winter ahead. The Shanes of this year are counting on us.

Small Shifts, Big Gifts

Think of your students this year. Can you think of one or two students who are your "Shanes"? This week, try to spend two uninterrupted minutes with them each day or do one small thing each day to help them feel seen and heard. At the end of the week, reflect to see if those conscious acts toward connection have made a positive impact in your teacher/student relationship.

Set a personal or professional goal for the week based on one small shift.

Weekly Win: At the end of the week, jot down one great thing that happened.

8

Want to Be Happier?
Start Here

We all want to be happy. In a perfect world, happiness would greet us each morning, usher us around, and surround our days with lovely things, moments, and people. But positive psychology tells us that the world isn't inherently positive or negative; it's neutral. What we put out into the universe undoubtedly impacts what comes back.

As the school year kicks into high gear, you have the capability to impact your own happiness. Although there may not be a linear list of steps to follow to become happier, there is a definite place to start. According to positive psychologists, the single most impactful practice that boosts optimism and happiness is *gratitude*.

When I first learned this, I was underwhelmed. That's it?! I just have to recognize and recall the good? I can do *that!*

In his 2020 book *STRIVE for Happiness in Education*, Rob Dunlop shares the work of Robert Emmons, a leading scientific expert on gratitude. Emmons claims that those who consistently practice gratitude "sleep better, have lower blood pressure, feel less isolated and become more outgoing and altruistic" (p. 131).

I can't imagine any of us wouldn't want to sleep better and feel more satisfied and connected to the world. To that end, here's how to apply the important practice of gratitude in three easy steps: Recognize, recall, and record.

Recognize

Any single happy experience may be *minimized* or *maximized* depending on how much attention is focused on it. It's really that simple. When something good happens today, *recognize* it. It could be the first sip of coffee in the morning, the colleague who made an extra set of copies so you didn't have to, the *aha* moment of a student finally "getting" long division, the funny thing your son said at dinner, an evening without commitments so everyone's home.

When we pay attention, scan for the good stuff, and *recognize* when it happens, we have the ability to rewire our brain. Citing the UCLA Mindful Awareness Research Center, Madhuleena Chowdhury (2019) notes, "Gratitude does change the neural structures in the brain, and make us feel happier and more content. Feeling grateful and appreciating others when they do something good for us triggers the 'good' hormones and regulates effective functioning of the immune system" (paras. 45–46). She goes on to say, "By consciously practicing gratitude, we can train the brain to attend selectively to positive emotions and thoughts, thus reducing anxiety and feelings of apprehension" (para. 68).

Recall and Record

It's worth repeating: *The happiness derived from any experience may be minimized or maximized depending on how much attention you pay to it.* And how do you give those positive moments more attention? You recall and record them! Grab a journal or use an app like Grateful or Happyfeed and record those happy moments. After you get into this habit, you will notice that your brain is more likely to "scan for the good" automatically, making your days happier. When you recall and record those experiences daily, you are reliving them and ending the day in a state of peace and positivity. Recalling them also increases the likelihood that your happy memory stays in your long-term memory. The best part? It takes 30 seconds or less.

Now bring this idea into your classroom. How empowering would it be if you could show your students that gratitude makes a significantly positive impact on their young lives? In many classrooms, it's a classroom habit to "End the Day Happy" by recalling three positive things that happened that day and recording them in a gratitude journal.

And yes, some days it may be challenging to recognize three positive things in a day. One day, a 3rd grade student stared at a blank page in his journal and didn't record a thing. I asked if he needed help, and he looked down and quietly replied, "Today was hard. I don't have anything for this book today."

I felt sad when he said this, but quickly recognized this was the greatest teachable moment of my day.

"Jack," I said, "when our days are hard and annoying, it's even more important to scan for the good. Let's get really small and find one teeny-tiny thing that went right today that made you grateful."

Still nothing. So we looked up at the daily schedule, and I asked him to think about his school day.

"You started with morning meeting, then math, after that was read-aloud, and then gym before social studies and lunch." After a lengthy pause he said, "I liked when we went outside for gym. It wasn't so hot that I got all sweaty."

He did it! This 3rd grader was scanning for the good, even on the days when things weren't great. If he could do this at the age of 9, just imagine how his life will be impacted if he can scan for the good when he's 29, 49, or 79.

If you can help your students understand the positive impact gratitude can have on their lives, you will grow a classroom of rational optimists—and I can't think of anything better. (See Figure 8.1 for some gratitude journal sentence starters.)

Are you interested in spreading gratitude to your colleagues? Check out what our education association does with our interoffice mail (1,200 employees across 23 schools) to recognize and express gratitude. We each send an "intentional act of gratitude"

Figure 8.1 Gratitude Journal Sentence Starters

I am grateful for . . .

I am thankful for . . .

Today was a good day because . . .

I liked today because . . .

Today was fun when . . .

I am happy because . . .

I appreciate . . .

I'm so lucky because . . .

I love _____ because . . .

I'm thankful I learned . . .

---

to a colleague, thanking them for what they bring to the profession and encouraging them to pass it on by sending their own note of gratitude to one or two colleagues. It takes less than three minutes to do and will be remembered by both the writer and the recipient!

I've been keeping gratitude journals since 1999, and I'm convinced this practice contributes to my high happiness baseline. Five years ago, I found another fun way to record times of gratitude and happiness in 30 seconds or less: Gretchen Rubin's *Happiness Project One-Sentence Journal* (Rubin, 2009b). It's so great because it lets you archive five years of happy moments, but you only get a tiny bit of space, so you have to recognize, recall, and record only the best of the best stuff. Here's an example from my journal:

> 2018: Watching Pat be the best Dad ever playing catch with Ryan and jumping on the trampoline; laughing around the campfire at our multigenerational book club
>
> 2019: A pizza dinner at the Keenans'; sitting on the porch talking with Liz

2020: Zoom call with Liz, Jackie, and Brian to wish Nan a happy 88th birthday

2021: Lindsay, Jason, Michele, and Brian taking me to an impromptu happy hour and calling it "Make Suzanne Happy Day"; Jenn surprising Emerson and me with Rita's; wine from Nichole on the porch

2022: Laughing about bidet jokes with Lisa, Bryan, and Charlene (I have very funny friends)

I've heard from people who purchased a copy of this journal for their child when they began high school or college as a way to archive the good stuff in a new journey. I like to give people a copy on milestone birthdays as a new season is ushered in. When I travel, I keep a list of the moments I am grateful for in my notes app so I can record them in my journal when I get home.

Already a Gratitude Guru?

If gratitude is already a daily practice for you, consider using your strength in a new way. I try to flex my gratitude muscles when I introduce people to one another. Instead of saying, "Corinne, this is Bev; Bev, meet Corinne," for example, I might say, "Corinne, this is my friend Bev. I am so grateful for her because she encourages me to squeeze the heck out of every day. And Bev, this is Corinne. She is such a gift because she teaches me how to acknowledge the simple beauty in every situation." Introducing special people conscientiously grounded in gratitude puts positivity into a neutral universe. And guess what? Happiness abounds for everyone involved.

During joyful seasons in my life, gratitude flourishes. During challenging seasons, gratitude helps me sift through what's in front of me to discern my next right thing. It anchors just about everything in my personal and professional life.

You've heard the phrase "seeing is believing"; now consider the opposite: *believing is seeing.* If you believe the world is ultimately good and that your life abounds with people and things to be grateful for, that is what you will train your mind and heart to see.

Believing is seeing. What a great place to begin!

TEACH
HAPPIER

Small Shifts, Big Gifts

Can you commit to jotting down at least one thing you are grateful for each day this week? Can you envision your students doing the same in the classroom? See if this practice of gratitude increases your overall happiness at school or at home.

Set a personal or professional goal for the week based on one small shift.

Weekly Win: At the end of the week, jot down one great thing that happened.

TEACH HAPPIER
LESSON

Objective: Students will learn how gratitude boosts long-term happiness and begin keeping a gratitude journal.

Procedure

1. Read/summarize this week's chapter. If you want to add some additional information, you can share a Harvard Medical School case study (Stickgold et al., 2020) in which participants played Tetris every day for 30 days. After about a week and a half, they started to see Tetris shapes everywhere (in the sky, in the cereal aisle, etc.). What does this teach us? We can train our brain regarding what it sees! (Note: I learned about this case study and its implications on conditioning our minds from Shawn Achor's *The Happiness Advantage* [2010)].)

2. Ask students, "How can we train our brain to see what is good?" Then share the answer: by recognizing, recalling, and recording the good things in our life.

3. Model how to create a gratitude journal. Use the sentence starters from Figure 8.1 to write two or three entries.

4. Encourage students to begin their journal. If they would like to share, you can highlight the fact that most things we're grateful for are quite simple.

5. After a few weeks of practicing gratitude, gauge student reaction. Ask students, "Has this practice helped increase your overall happiness? How?"

9

Be a Part of Your Own Rescue

I heard something the other day that was so interesting that it has been swirling in my mind ever since. It's about whitewater rafting. Apparently, the first rule of whitewater rafting is that if you end up off the raft and in the water, you must "be a part of your own rescue." You have to figure out what you need yourself. Can you swim to shore? Climb back onto the raft? Grab the paddle?

You must *be a part of your own rescue*. What a metaphor!

You are now in Week 9 of learning more about yourself and what helps you feel more content, aligned, and balanced. Now that you have some important background knowledge, you can be a part of your own rescue in your personal or professional life by determining what tiny 2-degree shifts you can make in your thoughts, language, or actions that can aid in your rescue when you are tossed off your own metaphorical raft.

Here's how "be a part of your own rescue" recently manifested for me. It was Sunday morning, and I felt that Sunday morning panic many adults feel: "Argh, I have to squeeze 100 hours of all the things into one day—how in the world will it all get done?" The visible home and school workload (combined with the phantom workload of office politics and challenging people) just felt like too much.

My next right thing was to quiet that hurried thought and calmly walk downstairs, pour a cup of coffee in my favorite mug, and scroll through the PostSecret website like I do every Sunday morning, which helped me exhale and center myself. Just a few minutes later, my son asked for pancakes, so I scuffed into the kitchen and started mixing up the batter. I looked around my quiet house, and everyone in my family was just kind of relaxing and enjoying themselves. Don't get me wrong, I love a relaxed, happy family—but as I began to make the pancakes, I couldn't help but think about everything I needed to get done for school and home. And I started getting annoyed—at everything. Like to the point where I felt my family was relaxing *at* me (do I sense you nodding your head right now?).

Pancakes were on the table, and I begrudgingly grabbed my purse and ran to the grocery store. With every aisle I walked, I became increasingly annoyed, with this delightful script running on a loop in my head:

> I do everything around here. Wouldn't it be nice to just *sit
> around all day* and have this food magically appear in the
> fridge? I bet nobody will notice the laundry isn't started yet and
> I'll have to do it when I get back. Does anyone even notice all
> that I do, much less appreciate it? *All* of it! *Any* of it! The visible
> *and* invisible things! And I still have so much planning to do!

You can imagine the state I was in when I got home. As my kids would lovingly say, I was close to having a nutty.

I wanted to blame someone—anyone—for my situation. Why couldn't someone just *make it better?* Why couldn't they rescue me and make me happier? Right this very second?!

Because rescuing your mental state is an inside job, friend.

When you get off course and feel like you're drowning, you need to be a part of your own rescue, just like those rafters. You have to discern your next right thing to make things better.

That Sunday, I recognized I need to be a part of my own rescue. I couldn't wait for my husband or kids to understand what I needed and meet those needs, so I deliberately decided to break away from some of the to-dos and do something to actually make me feel better and improve the situation. I drank a glass of water to make sure I was hydrated. That helped a little. Then I went into the basement *all by myself* and worked out for a half-hour. Then I took a shower, making sure not to hurry.

I reentered my day at 11:16 a.m. I didn't feel like a whole new person, but I did feel a bit more balanced, aligned, and *calm*. I was able to move through my day with renewed perspective, energy, and patience. I just had to recognize that I needed to be a part of my own rescue in order to do that.

This strategy is applicable at work, too. Totally annoyed at a colleague? Desperate for the district to take something—anything—off your plate? You can't expect others to come to your rescue. You have to do that work yourself.

For example, recently at my own work, we were in the final stretch of another exhausting school year, and everyone was *D-O-N-E*. Tired. Over it. As we all limped toward the finish line, crossing off those final to-do items, everyone's patience had worn thin. I was fielding a lot of phone calls and answering questions when a conversation with a well-respected colleague became a little more charged than either of us would have wanted. Our exchange became curt, even a bit confrontational. When our phone call ended, I felt annoyed and upset by the way this colleague had spoken to me.

I then realized I had two choices: I could spend the next week nursing my grudge and feel upset when I saw him at an upcoming meeting. *Or* I could be a part of my own rescue and work to repair the potential damage done. I knew it would take work, but I also knew this was within my realm of influence and control.

After talking the situation through with my closest work friend, I made an uncomfortable phone call to this colleague. I was able to express my sadness and disappointment, and he was able to do the same. I told him I cared too much about our professional relationship to hold a grudge. This conversation was hard work, but those five minutes of discomfort freed up the space in my head and my heart that I needed to feel healthy and whole.

If I hadn't been a part of my own rescue, that initial contentious conversation would have taken up more real estate in my thoughts than it deserved. It would have compromised my time, energy, and contentment.

What is something you can do to protect your headspace and your sanity? Often, it's just one of those small shifts in thought, language, or action that help to accomplish this.

Be a part of your own rescue.

Small Shifts, Big Gifts

How good are you at being a part of your own rescue? Think about the small, 2-degree shifts you have started to incorporate in your personal or professional life. What are things you do that help you feel more content, aligned, and balanced? If you are stuck, you may want to revisit some of the things that you said made you happy in Week 5. The ultimate goal is to *access these shifts* when you need to be a part of your own rescue!

Set a personal or professional goal for the week based on one small shift.

Weekly Win: At the end of the week, jot down one great thing that happened.

10

Wake Up for Bedtime

The other morning, I was listening to an interview with Dr. Edith Eger on an episode of Brené Brown's *Unlocking Us* podcast (Brown, 2021b). Dr. Eger is a brilliant psychologist and author in her 90s who often shares about her heartbreaking experience in the Holocaust and what she has learned from it. Dr. Eger says that the choices we have in our lives are some of the greatest gifts we'll ever have because, ultimately, those little choices determine so much.

As I made lunches for my kids and listened to sweet Edith's wise words before the sun came up, she said something I can't stop thinking about: "I choose in the morning how I am going to feel at night."

I choose in the morning how I am going to feel at night.

I put down the strawberries and ran to record this brilliant idea in my notes app because I found it so profound. It got me thinking: Can we really decide in the morning how we are going to feel at night? Is that realistic in real life?

So I put Dr. Eger's idea to the test. And guess what? It works.

After the lunches were packed, I decided that, when I went to bed that night, I would feel three things: accomplished, proud, and fulfilled.

I went into the basement for a 30-minute workout. I pushed myself for one more rep—and I felt proud and accomplished.

When I got to work, I decided to reframe my thinking about something I struggle with: I can get annoyed when I am repeatedly interrupted at work. Though it is rare for me to be in my office, if I *am* there, chances are I'll get a lot of visitors. I *love* the people I work with, but when I'm "in the zone," I can get flustered if that time is repeatedly interrupted. I've tried to be more tolerant for years and I honestly haven't gotten much better at it.

In an effort to live into my intention, I went back to Dr. Eger's advice and chose to see those interruptions as *opportunities to connect.* This kept me curious and engaged during the inevitable interruptions, helping me feel proud and fulfilled by the stronger connection I created with colleagues.

That afternoon while I was teaching, I noticed that a student who is usually energetic and animated seemed withdrawn and sad. I ended the lesson a few minutes early so I could check in with her individually. She shared a few things that were making life challenging for her. We hugged, and I knew how I could follow up and keep my eye on her. And yep: After that three-minute check-in, I felt accomplished, proud, and fulfilled.

On my way home after school, I needed a few extra minutes in the silence of my car to recharge before tending to my family. Fulfillment.

All day I kept thinking, "Suzanne, how do you want to feel when you climb in your bed to read and end the day?" When I anchored myself to this intention, my day felt lighter, more meaningful. I was far more engaged and present in each moment at school and at home.

This story exemplifies rational optimism: understanding there are a few things that are out of your control, but realizing those few things are finite, and you can positively impact 80 to 90 percent of what happens in your life. The practice of choosing in the morning how you are going to feel at night sets you up perfectly for harnessing that 80 to 90 percent.

As the late neurologist and psychiatrist Viktor E. Frankl (2006) said, "Everything can be taken from a man but one thing: the last of the human freedoms—to choose one's attitude in any given set of circumstances, to choose one's own way" (p. 66).

Every day you wake up in the morning and go to sleep at night. What you choose to do in between is what matters most.

Small Shifts, Big Gifts

Keep your eyes on your own paper as you scan for the good and scan for the wins! Each day this week, acknowledge something you have done to help your home family, your classroom family, or yourself to grow. Remember, these do not have to be revolutionary shifts—just those that helped move things in a positive direction. When you train your brain to look for the wins *on your own paper*, the likelihood of doing more good things in the future increases.

Set a personal or professional goal for the week based on one small shift.

Weekly Win: At the end of the week, jot down one great thing that happened.

REPORT
CARD

1

We do not learn from experience.
We learn from reflecting on experience.

— John Dewey —

You've made it to Week 10! Now is the time to take a breath, reflect on what you've learned these past few weeks, and direct your next small shifts in thoughts, language, and actions.

Review and summarize what was meaningful to you during the last 10 weeks.

1. Your Legacy Begins This Week
2. You Will Be Remembered for the Way You Love
3. Work/Life Satisfaction
4. Rational Optimism
5. Happiness Is a Discipline
6. The Importance of *You*
7. Sideline Conversations
8. Want to Be Happier? Start Here
9. Be a Part of Your Own Rescue
10. Wake Up for Bedtime

Reflections

Scan for the good! Review your Weekly Wins. What is something that makes you proud or especially happy? Are these Weekly Wins helping you tell the story you recorded in the "Before You Begin" chapter on page 7?

Name one or two small shifts you've incorporated in your personal or professional life that have made a positive impact at work and/ or at home. These may be shifts you want to incorporate long term. Can you articulate the impact of these small shifts in your life?

Name one or two small shifts you didn't have the bandwidth for earlier but want to practice soon. What do you hope to accomplish by incorporating these small shifts in your personal or professional life?

Look back to your original happiness baseline (see Figure i.1 on p. 6). Overall, are you feeling more content and aligned now? If so, describe how. If not, consider what small shifts in thoughts, language, or actions could help you feel an increase in your overall happiness at work or at home.

Where would you place yourself on the happiness continuum today? If possible, jot down a few reasons why.

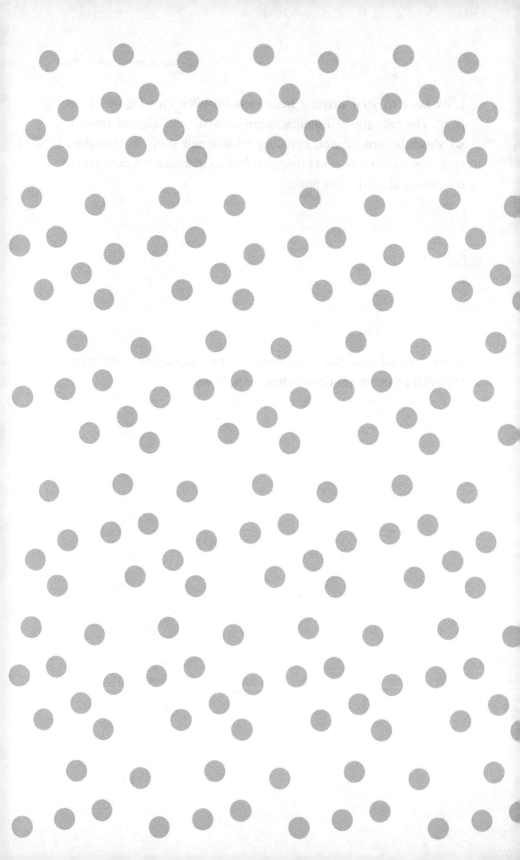

2

"We spend a lot of time up in our own head. We might as well make it nice up there."

— Kelly Corrigan —

11

Finding the Magic

I flew across the country to compete on *Wheel of Fortune* and won $12,600. That's a pretty good story, right? Actually, it's when the wheel stopped spinning and the cameras stopped rolling that the real story began.

I left Sony Studios so excited that I forgot to retrieve my driver's license first. When I returned to reclaim it, I was greeted at the security gate by Lewis (his name has been changed), an employee who was to take me back to the set on his golf cart.

Lewis accelerated quickly, and I learned that he was a happy, energetic gentleman. "Suzanne, I saw the whole show," he said. "You were so much fun to watch! You said you're a teacher, right?"

"Yes," I replied.

"Do you ever work with students with special learning needs?"

"Yes."

"OK, then. You and I are going to take the long way back to get your things. I want to tell you a story. When I was 5 years old, I was adopted from a reservation. I couldn't read. I couldn't write. Things were hard—really hard. I never went to school before, and when my parents finally got me there, I couldn't do a lot of the things the other kids could do." As Lewis shared his childhood experiences, tears quietly came to the corners of his eyes.

"Nobody could figure me out, but they knew something was wrong with me. That's how they said it, too. They said that something was *wrong* with me."

He paused to take a deep breath before continuing. "But then, I met my 3rd grade teacher, and she held my shoulders, looked into my eyes, and said, 'Lewis, there is magic in you and I am going to find it.'

"So she worked with me. A lot. She kept reminding me that she promised to find the magic, and she never gave up on me. Never once. You know what she figured out? That I had dyslexia, and that was something not many people talked about back then. So after she learned more about dyslexia, she figured out how to teach me how to read and write! And then guess what? She made sure that my *4th* grade teacher could teach me the way I learned, and then my *5th* grade teacher."

The golf cart stopped.

"Look at me now, Suzanne. Here I am driving this cart around Sony Studios, meeting wonderful people, making plenty of money, and I've connected myself with others in the business. I'm doing everything I've always wanted to do. And it's because of my 3rd grade teacher. She found the magic in me that nobody else could."

I quickly found myself hugging someone I'd met less than five minutes earlier, whispering, "Thank you for sharing this with me, Lewis." We dried our eyes and shared a comforting smile, and I continued: "Teachers need to hear stories like yours because we often don't know the impact that we make on our students. As public schoolteachers, we get criticized often, and when that happens, it is so easy to lose sight of what matters most. I promise to go home and share this story with my colleagues who work hard to find the magic in their students."

"Please tell them," he said. "And tell them I say thank you."

I told him I would. And years later, the conversation we shared in that golf cart has eclipsed what happened in the *Wheel of Fortune* studio—really!

One of my favorite authors, Glennon Doyle, said in a talk I attended, "Teachers are the first responders, the front line, the disconnection detectives. What you do in those classrooms when no one is watching is our best hope" (2018).

We are hardworking, dedicated teachers who sometimes need to be reminded that our work matters. Our tired eyes may not see the proof of our work and dedication as often as we would like, but it is there if we look for it.

And if we look close enough, we may even find some undiscovered magic.

TEACH
HAPPIER

Small Shifts, Big Gifts

Pick a student—maybe one who is a little quieter and can blend in relatively unnoticed. Can you find the magic in them and let them know? When you share that positivity with someone else, your happiness levels will increase, too!

Set a personal or professional goal for the week based on one small shift.

Weekly Win: At the end of the week, jot down one great thing that happened.

12

What's Your Weekend Wish?

A few weeks ago, I ran an after-school workshop. It was a cold winter Thursday, already dark shortly after 4:30 p.m., and we were downright weary. To rally the group, I started with a routine I like to call "Let's Start This Thing Happy," where we take two minutes to prime our tired teacher brains with something positive.

"What is one thing you are looking forward to this weekend?" I asked.

Responses ranged from "I'll see my son's basketball tournament" to "My family is visiting from out of town" to "I have book club tomorrow night and I know I will laugh the entire time."

All perfectly expected responses, until one colleague nearing the end of her teaching career spoke up.

"My husband and I treat every weekend like a spa weekend," she blissfully shared. "We wear fuzzy robes, make mimosas, order in delicious food, and relax for the entire weekend."

Everyone looked at me. Then they looked at one another. And then they let out a collective sigh: This did not sound like the weekends the rest of us were experiencing.

Robes? Luxury? Turn our home into a temporary spa? I am in a pretty busy season, and I imagine you are, too. I usually spend my weekends shuffling my two kids around, running countless errands, trying to get my family of four ready for the upcoming week in 48 hours or less. It's tiring to even *type* those facts.

But I could come up with 100 other reasons not to create special moments on the weekends that break up the monotony or slow their frenzied pace. I learned from this colleague who made it her business to create space for what gave her joy that it's on us to take charge of our time. If we don't *prioritize*, *preserve*, and *protect* our time, our weekend can turn into a hurried blur filled with lots of tasks and little joy.

If we can manage to *weekend happier*, it will help us *teach happier*, *parent happier*, *partner happier*, and *friend happier*. To get started, ask yourself: "What is my weekend wish?"

One small shift my husband and I have made is to ask this question together every Wednesday or Thursday night. It gives us a chance to envision what we need to feel reenergized, rested, and rejuvenated by the weekend. Oftentimes it is a fairly small wish: going for a long run on Saturday, grabbing a coffee with Kristin to catch up, being alone and just reading for an hour.

It takes us less than a minute to decide our weekend wish. And when the wish later turns into action, it honors what we need. It's an opportunity to vocalize a need and then *commit* to meeting it.

If it's "one of those weeks" and I feel tired by Tuesday I will ask, "What do I want/need to do with my time this weekend to regroup and rejuvenate?" According to positive psychology, when we have something to look forward to, whether in the short term or long term, we become happier; thinking about the future can make us feel better in the present. This effect can actually be measured through brain imaging. "[A]nticipating something positive actually helps to maintain dopamine levels in your brain," shares marriage and family therapist Kimberly Diggles (quoted in Volpe, 2020). "Just the idea of anticipating something good can physically change your brain chemistry so you feel happy" (para. 7). Once again, we are reminded that we have tremendous influence on our own levels of happiness.

Gretchen Rubin (2007) encourages us to ask ourselves, "If your life is a parade of obligations, dreaded tasks, and mandatory appearances, take a minute to figure out something you would find fun . . . and start anticipating it."

We *find* time for what we have to do. But we need to *make* time for what we *want* to do. We must make time for ourselves so we can get back into our classrooms Monday morning feeling more energized than we did when we staggered out Friday afternoon.

All we have is time. So here's to squeezing the heck out of our weekends and showing up for our students at school and families at home every other day of the week.

TEACH
HAPPIER

Small Shifts, Big Gifts

How can you proactively add some positivity into the time and space you have this upcoming weekend? Make a weekend wish—imagine it, share it, and plan for it!

Set a personal or professional goal for the week based on one small shift.

Weekly Win: At the end of the week, jot down one great thing that happened.

TEACH HAPPIER
LESSON

Objective: Students will create a weekend wish and see if it helps them feel rejuvenated for the upcoming week.

Procedure
1. Ask students if they ever feel overscheduled or overcommitted during the weekend.
2. Ask students how they would want to feel on Monday morning if they could wave a magic wand.
3. Model how you will plan to do something this weekend that will make you feel more aligned and rejuvenated for the following week. Try to make it something students can relate to.
4. Have students prioritize one thing they want to create time and space for this weekend. (This may connect to the "Happiness Is a Discipline" lesson from Week 5!)
5. On Monday, discuss this practice with students to see if it made a positive impact not only on their weekend but also on how they are feeling as they enter a new week in school.

13

What Could Go *Right?*

I don't know about you, but when I'm in the full swing of the school routine, I sometimes let my guard down and just expect things to roll on as automatically as possible. But as a rational optimist, I'm not just going to close my eyes, cross my fingers, and hope that everything will be rainbows and unicorns. Not a chance. I know hope is not a plan. What I *will* do is anticipate good things happening and train my brain to notice when things are going right.

Train my brain? Yes, it's possible!

Neuroscientists and neurobiologists continue to teach us that our brains are malleable and every experience or thought literally changes our brain.

The other day I was listening to a sermon by Dr. Robert Linders, theologian in residence at St. Paul's Lutheran Church in our beautiful little town of Doylestown, Pennsylvania. "Any set of circumstances," he said, "is a mix of outer facts and inner attitude."

Let's hear that again: *Any set of circumstances is a mix of outer facts and inner attitude.*

Have you ever had days that fall apart right from the get-go? Of course—it happens to all of us. The other day, by 8:02 a.m., I had realized the following things: that I'd forgotten my laptop charger at home (and my laptop was at 8 percent), that I'd left my cup of coffee on the kitchen counter, and that a student was leaving for vacation *tomorrow* and needed a week's worth of work for our writing group. I am sure you have had mornings just like this. When we do, usually the first thing we'll ask our family or colleagues is "What else can go wrong?!"—and unfortunately, once you ask that question, chances are things will only get worse.

OK, but what about those days when things are just good? That's what our little story this week is about—a random Tuesday morning just a few weeks ago. I won't take you through the whole day, but I'll walk you through the very beginning. It went a little like this.

First thing in the morning, I came downstairs to get a cup of coffee at the *exact moment* the pot finished brewing—*and* my favorite mug was clean.

I noticed that my husband had *folded the laundry from last night.*

There were exactly *two* blueberry bagels left—one for each of my kids. (Yes, that's a pretty big deal here at Camp Dailey.)

I heard my favorite Zac Brown song on my way to work (and sang it at the top of my lungs, thank you very much).

I stopped to get gas, and my phone fell out of the car without my noticing. A kind stranger gently beeped his horn to let me know.

As I noticed all these small but glorious things happening, I thought to myself, "Today is going to be a great day. The universe is going to lay everything out for me today exactly the way it's supposed to be. What else could go *right?*"

And guess what happened?

Throughout that random Tuesday, I noticed so many things: the copier was available when I needed it, the student who usually resists reading happily invested in a book, a green light was perfectly timed. It wasn't a special day by anybody's definition. It was just a regular Tuesday. But I'll tell you this: The moment I thought, "What else could go right?" a lot of things started to do just that. It made me feel lucky.

Psychology professor Dr. Richard Wiseman (2003) has extensively researched the idea of luck. He conducted a famous experiment where he asked people if they thought they were lucky or unlucky. When he put a $20 bill on the sidewalk, those who noticed it considered themselves lucky. "The key to good luck is an open mind," he concluded. "Unlucky people miss chance opportunities because they are too focused on looking for something else. Lucky people are more relaxed and open, and therefore see what is there rather than just what they are looking for."

Wiseman's study reaffirms Dr. Linders's notion that any set of circumstances is a mix of outer facts and inner attitude.

In his sermon, Dr. Linders also shared that the greatest difference among people lies in what they *anticipate*. We subconsciously choose our emotion when we set our expectation. This week, your invitation is to anticipate good things and notice when your day is going well. And when you do that, ask yourself, "What else could go right?" It's an immediate adjustment to help you feel more aligned.

If your day is going off the rails, re-anchor yourself and shift from the automatic "What else could go wrong?" to "What could go right?" and see if your expectations impact your perspective and perception.

Small Shifts, Big Gifts

TEACH
HAPPIER

This week, anticipate that things are going to go right and see if that makes a measurable difference to your levels of rational optimism.

Set a personal or professional goal for the week based on one small shift.

Weekly Win: At the end of the week, jot down one great thing that happened.

14

December Is the New August

Depending on when you started this book, it's either December already or will be soon. For a moment, travel back a few months to August—sunny, relaxing, all-the-time-in-the-world August. Remember enjoying your lunch and not inhaling it in under seven minutes? Using the bathroom *any time you wanted?* Leisurely sipping *hot* coffee from a *real mug?* Chances are you were an amazing version of yourself in August: rested, optimistic, happy.

Now here you are in December—cold, hectic, can't-get-it-all-done-in-a-day December. Perhaps the December version of yourself is not as rested, optimistic, and happy as your August self. But, friend, I have good news: Winter break is almost here.

How do we squeeze the heck out of our winter break so we can make December the new August? By prioritizing three things: your *people*, your *space*, and your *word*.

Your People

According to Shawn Achor (2010), social support is a far greater predictor of happiness than any other factor. Anecdotally, I, too, have found that 100 percent of happy people have one thing in common: *strong social relationships*. However, like me, you may have recently sent a text to a friend that goes something like this: "Sorry I haven't been around much lately—things have been crazy. Just checking in to see how you're doing. Let's try to get together soon." We aren't bad friends, just busy teachers, and this is a hectic time for us.

With the gift of time and space this winter break, you can nurture your personal and professional relationships. Schedule the lunch or coffee date, the small-group walk, the date night, the dinner where you can laugh into the evening hours (on a weeknight!) to reconnect with those who strengthen you in your personal life.

Although you may want distance from your teaching life this break, consider scheduling something with someone at school you want to connect or reconnect with. Investing in your professional relationships while on winter break will help you feel more balanced and supported as you usher in another busy season in January.

Your Space

Are you ready for a good laugh? Remember in August laying out your (ironed!) clothes *the night before school* and, when packing your work bag, *actually placing your pens in the pockets designed to hold them?* Bless. I mean, we were a real sight just a few months ago. Our December selves are happy if we have a working pen in our bag and our clothes are appropriate for the weather.

In her book *Outer Order, Inner Calm* (2020), Gretchen Rubin teaches us that our *inner* calm is undoubtedly connected to our *outer* calm. Think about the spaces that you can reorganize to create inner calm: the closet; the dining room table covered in holiday cards, receipts, and single gloves; the side compartments in the car; that disheveled school bag. Your level of organization in August made you outwardly prepared for the tasks ahead, and during this break, you can again proactively organize important spaces to protect your inner calm at the cusp of the new year.

Your Word

Winter is the time when we think about our New Year's resolutions. *This year I want to emphasize relationships. This year I will prioritize peace. This year my students and I will encourage one another to be creative.* Too often, these vows are quieted as the hustle and bustle of the school year ramp up. Recognize and renew the energy of your resolution in December, before you flip the calendar. Doing this can

help build perspective before you return to your classroom family—
and help ensure that you keep your word.

So go for it—recapture your sunny August self during the cold
month of December by prioritizing your people, your space, and
your word.

Reflect. Recalibrate. Reclaim your August self.

December is the new August.

Small Shifts, Big Gifts

TEACH HAPPIER

How can you make this December the new August? Consider ways you can connect with a *person*, organize your *space*, and reinforce your *word* with this glorious unstructured time!

Set a personal or professional goal for the week based on one small shift.

Weekly Win: At the end of the week, jot down one great thing that happened.

15

Grown-Ups Need to Have Fun

Here you are in Week 15. You are established in your routines and daily life at school. Things may start to feel a bit boring. Mundane. You may find yourself moving through your days automatically, without much thought. The other day I couldn't remember if it was Tuesday or Wednesday; there was nothing special about what was happening now or what lay ahead in the near future that made it clear what day it was.

As you've moved through this book, you've been invited to celebrate some of the ways you show up in the world for yourself and others. This week, I'm going to ask you to *not* show up.

Stay with me.

Think back to a time when you just had a lot of fun—the more specific the example, the better.

A recent example in my life would be the time I spent with my three girlfriends on what we affectionately call "nook night." About every other month or so, my dear friend Jenny, who is an amazing cook, makes a delicious meal, and my two other dear friends and I show up in yoga pants, ponytails, and sweatshirts. Kristin, Leanne, Jenny, and I enjoy drinks and food in Jenny's dining room (which we call the nook). The nook somehow does not get internet service, which just adds to the magic of it all. We laugh and eat and laugh and talk and laugh and drink.

I just adore this bimonthly nook night. It's like a younger version of *The Golden Girls*. Time goes by so quickly, like we're in some kind of time warp. Every single time I leave a nook night, I feel fulfilled and lighter inside. It's just so much *fun*.

We often tell ourselves that we don't have time for fun because there is just so much to *do*. But neuroscience and psychology now tell us that if we want to have more mental space for higher productivity, we have to make space for fun. As author and researcher Martha Beck notes, "Having fun is not a diversion from a successful life; it is the pathway to it" (2002). She continues:

> Each of us is born with a propensity to have fun doing certain types of activities, in certain proportions—you may love doing something I hate and vice versa. I call the pattern of activities you most enjoy your "funprint," and like your thumbprint it's unique. It seems obvious to me (and research backs me up) that we are most productive, persistent, creative, and flexible when we're engaged in precisely the combination of activities that brings us maximum fun. Your funprint isn't a frivolous indulgence. It is the map of your true life, an instruction manual for your essential purpose, written in the language of joy. Learning to read and respond to it is one of the most crucial things you'll ever do. (para. 2)

My beloved nook night is a funprint. Hours go by, and what do I accomplish? Not a single thing. Nothing gets cleaned, nothing gets marked off the to-do list, nothing gets tightened or toned, lesson plans don't get written—nothing but *fun* occurs. And you know what? This nook night fun gives me the energy I need in the next days to actually accomplish the things I have to accomplish as a 42-year-old grown-up.

Recently on Glennon Doyle's *We Can Do Hard Things* podcast (2022), guest Luvvie Ajayi Jones said that we know friendships are good for us when we feel like they are "charging stations" for our hearts and spirits. And that's exactly what nook nights are for me. The laughs and conversations we have within the dining room walls give me the energy for all the things outside those walls.

If you are a parent, I want to share one of the parenting goals Pat and I have. We want our son and daughter to know that being a grown-up can be *fun*. We don't want them to think that after they work hard and get a good job they'll face nothing but work, errands, chores, and tasks. *Gah!*

Rather, we want them to see that, after they work hard and get a fulfilling job, they get to *also* have fun with friends, go interesting places, and do fun things. It may sound silly that it's a priority at Camp Dailey, but it really is. I mean, every single year they see us get excited and prepare for an annual family event we host at our home. For 13 years now, our beloved cousins and friends come to our home for a day of outdoor games before we go off on an in-town pub crawl. The memories we make with our family and friends on this day (although sometimes fuzzy to recall) are some of the funniest and most cherished memories of the entire year. We want our kids to see that there are times when we can put some responsibilities aside and just have fun. *That* is worth working toward!

If boisterous games and a pub crawl aren't your thing, a nook night might be more your speed. Maybe it's a quiet night at home with Netflix and pizza, or a walk and talk at a nearby park with a friend. However you want to infuse fun just for fun's sake is up to you—what's important is prioritizing the time and space to do so.

Can we accomplish this at work, too? Oh yes, we can! I try to make it a point to schedule myself to be in a classroom at one of our buildings when they have their "Fat Friday" once a month. Departments take turns all year long filling the faculty room with crockpots, desserts, and snacks. When staff members walk into the faculty room, they are tossing away their calorie count for the day, but more important, they are also tossing aside the stresses and worries from the classroom. It's loud. There is laughing. People can connect with one another. Nothing gets checked off the checklist. Nothing gets graded. No emails are sent. It's just plain fun.

This week, I invite you to think about the people, settings, or activities that you find fun and thoughtfully plan to squeeze some of that fun into your personal or professional life. What can you do this week that honors play? What could be just plain fun? What could fulfill you and make you feel lighter inside? How can you show up for nothing else but your joy?

TEACH
HAPPIER

Small Shifts, Big Gifts

Think about the people, settings, or activities that help you find *fun*. How can you thoughtfully plan for some fun in your upcoming week?

Set a personal or professional goal for the week based on one small shift.

Weekly Win: At the end of the week, jot down one great thing that happened.

16

Plan Happier

Walking (or dare I say *gliding*) out of school and into the parking lot on Fridays is euphoric; walking (or dare I say *trudging*) into school on Mondays is not. As educators, we have all been living a Monday–Friday school week since we were 5 years old. Perhaps it's time to consider a small shift in how we think about our weeks.

If you were a day of the workweek, what day would you be? I would be a Tuesday. I generally feel rested and in the groove on Tuesdays. On a Tuesday morning around 10 a.m., I can accomplish *allll* the things.

Take a moment to think about which day of the week you feel most productive, rested, and happy.

Now that you have your day in mind, consider a small shift in thought. I no longer plan my weeks with a Monday–Friday mindset. Since my favorite workday is Tuesday, I instead use a Tuesday–Tuesday framework. This has helped make my weeks more productive and fulfilling while also decreasing my Sunday Scaries.

Here's how this looks. My goal is to have what I need for the upcoming week (Tuesday–Tuesday) as prepared as realistically possible. At work, I'm looking ahead to lessons, presentations, meetings, and deadlines and prioritizing my to-do list. Comparing my energy level on Tuesdays versus Sundays is downright laughable. I am much more realistic and focused when I plan and begin accomplishing tasks on a Tuesday. And if I stay a bit later on a

Tuesday, it feels better than trying to cram everything into a panicked Sunday evening.

This shift helps me at home, too. On Tuesdays, my daughter is at a barn riding her horse and my son is typically on a basketball court, so there's a chunk of time when they are doing their thing and I have the energy and space to do mine. For example, Tuesday afternoon and evening is when I'll figure out what the rest of the humans in my home are eating for the next few days and get to the grocery store. (Bonus points if I can get there on my way home from work.) Sunday grocery stores are busy and stressful and *ugh*. Maximizing this time on Tuesday helps us feel replenished and settled.

Not only does this rhythm seem to work for me during the week, but it also opens up a bit more space in my head and heart on the weekends so I can truly enjoy that time with my family and friends and enter Monday feeling rested and ready.

Your invitation this week is to consider whether this kind of shift could work for you. On which weekday do you feel at your best? It may be worth exploring how to adjust your weekly time frame so that you can proceed through your days feeling both accomplished and settled.

You don't have to be trudging into school on Monday mornings. Plan happier instead.

Small Shifts, Big Gifts

On which weekday are you at your best? Consider shifting the way you look at your upcoming week to see if it helps you feel more rested and ready next week.

Set a personal or professional goal for the week based on one small shift.

Weekly Win: At the end of the week, jot down one great thing that happened.

17

Just Say No

It's in educators' DNA to be helpers. We're here to support, give, and nurture. It's our greatest gift—but it can also be our biggest weakness.

Why? Because all this supporting, giving, and nurturing can be downright exhausting. Too often, we disregard our own needs in our efforts to help others.

Just the other day, my good friend was racing through the hallway trying to get to her mailbox, grab her lunch, and text her husband a quick update before the bell rang. She is a beautiful person and always well put together and accessorized, but truth be told, she looked pretty haggard (no, I didn't tell her this).

I speed-walked with her and asked her how I could help. "I need everyone to leave me alone so I can sleep for four days straight," she said. "I helped run this morning's faculty meeting, I just met with my mentee to help him prepare for parent conferences, today after school I am running the yoga club, and then I have to work on my son's basketball fundraiser."

I tilted my head to the side and looked at her like, "You're doing too much."

"I know, I know," she replied. "You know me, though. I can't say no. It will be fine. It's just a lot right now."

It's easy to relate to her, right? In my first year of teaching in a new district, my 4th grade students were "buddies" with a class of 2nd grade students. We would get together about once a month and do something fun related to holidays or help our buddies with a reading or writing project. As we neared the holidays, the 2nd grade teacher and I thought it would be fun to make gingerbread houses with the students (let's observe a moment of silence for our young, energetic, and unrealistic hearts). At this time, my brand-new husband of one month was on a nine-month assignment living in Arkansas, so I only saw him every other weekend. But my colleague *really wanted to make homemade gingerbread* on a Sunday when my husband was home.

Would you believe I couldn't say no to her?

I left my husband, my bulldog, a Buffalo Bills game, and my sanity at home while I went to her house to make gingerbread. It took hours. I was sad the whole time and resented it altogether. For some reason, I just couldn't say no.

We all find ourselves in these predicaments when our minds and hearts are yelling, "No!" but somehow our voice says, "Sure, we can do that." The moment we commit to something that will not ultimately serve us, we start feeling sad or frustrated.

I am happy to report that, 20 years of teaching later, I am getting better at navigating these situations. When I find myself feeling run-down as I try to help everyone at school or at home, that's a signal for me to say no to something. I know this can be very hard; it's taken me years of practice. I'm still not great at it, but here are a few ways I say no:

- "Sorry, I can't."

- "Thanks for the invitation, but that isn't going to work for us."

- "I wish I could help, but I won't be able to."

Did you notice anything about those responses? I said no. Period. Without any explanation. I didn't need an excuse that would satisfy the person who was asking. I needed a response that was going to satisfy my wellness.

Did you notice what I *didn't* do? I didn't say yes and commit to something, then worry for hours or days about how I was going to get out of that thing at the last minute. That takes up way too much real estate in my head and heart and makes me feel unaligned and discontent.

Just say no. Period.

Do you know what happens when we begin to say no to the things we really don't want to do? We create time and space for the things we love to do. Things that energize our minds and bodies. Time and space? Sign me up!

Here's to saying yes to saying no.

TEACH
HAPPIER

Small Shifts, Big Gifts

Think about clearing a bit of headspace or heartspace by feeling that it's OK to say no to something without elaborating or backtracking later. See if saying no to something contributes to your overall physical, mental, or emotional well-being.

Set a personal or professional goal for the week based on one small shift.

Weekly Win: At the end of the week, jot down one great thing that happened.

18

Even If . . .

Have you ever heard the quote "I am flexible as long as everything is exactly the way I want it"? How great is that? Do you, too, feel great discomfort when everything seems out of your control? Sometimes it's nearly impossible to feel like you have a firm grasp on things. This week, we will learn a small language shift that may help you lower your shoulders and breathe a bit deeper during this time of uncertainty. The best part is that it takes five seconds or less.

What If . . .

Often at around 3:30 a.m., a little voice awakens me. It sounds a little like this: "What if my document camera doesn't work when I'm being observed during math? What if my daughter struggles with her test? What if I have to sub tomorrow? What if the weather is bad and I have to cancel my trip to see my dad?"

If you also find your thoughts landing in the world of *what ifs*, you're not alone. I've found this to be pretty common among colleagues at every level.

As a rational optimist, I have made a small shift in language that has made all the difference. When that *what if* voice starts talking, I think, "I see you, *what if*, and I'll raise you one: *even if.*"

Does that sound crazy? It may at first. But look at what this small shift in language can do:

- *Even if* my document camera doesn't work during math, I can use chart paper to model the concept.

- *Even if* my daughter struggles with her test, we can talk about it when she comes home and share a blueberry muffin. I will remind her that grades are not as important as her wellness as we continue to navigate this postpandemic world.

- *Even if* I have to sub tomorrow, I can reschedule with colleagues and they will understand.

- *Even if* the weather is bad and the trip is canceled, Dad and I can FaceTime a few more times this month so we can still feel connected.

We may not be able to *control* much, but we can *influence* just about everything.

When we practice this language shift from *what if* to *even if*, we acknowledge the possible scenario and think about a possible response. This is just one more way we can harness that 80 to 90 percent of stuff that positive psychologists tell us is within our realm of influence and control. When we crave a sense of control, we aren't leaving it up to the universe to magically figure it out but, rather, thinking through what is within our realm of control to *respond* to that possibility.

So what if everything isn't exactly the way you want it? *Even if* it isn't, you can discern your next right thing with this simple shift in language.

Small Shifts, Big Gifts

TEACH HAPPIER

Try it! When you find yourself beginning a sentence with "What if," experiment with shifting it to "Even if" and see if that helps you gain a sense of control and calm.

Set a personal or professional goal for the week based on one small shift.

Weekly Win: At the end of the week, jot down one great thing that happened.

Objective: Students will be able to combat their worries by creating *even if* scenarios that they can apply in their lives at home or at school.

Procedure
1. Summarize the chapter for students.
2. Model a few ways you can get stuck in the *what ifs* and write them on the board.
3. Draw a vertical line near the *what ifs*. On the right-hand side of the line, change them all to *even ifs*.
4. Ask students: "What do you notice?"
5. Ask students: "How does changing our *what ifs* to *even ifs* help us?"
6. Have students write down at least two *what ifs* that they are experiencing in their lives. (Some examples from students have included "What if I fail my test?" "What if my dog runs out the front door when Amazon comes by?" "What if my sister doesn't keep her side of the room clean?" and "What if I can't get my homework done tonight?")
7. Guide students through changing their *what ifs* to *even ifs*. Encourage willing students to share with the class if they are comfortable doing so.
8. Discuss how this practice empowers us by focusing on what actions we can take when we begin to worry about something. Celebrate the fact that we are harnessing our 80 to 90 percent as rational optimists!

19

Do Less, Better

The other day, my husband and I were discussing how we felt like we were paying attention to 100 things all the time. By focusing on so many things, we kind of felt like we weren't *really* paying attention to anything. Our minds and hearts were equally weary.

I am sure you can relate. It just doesn't feel good.

As a rational optimist, I understand I can't control what the world is going to throw at me. But I *can* control what I pay attention to—what gets my time and, more important, what *doesn't* get my time.

Have you ever exercised with someone who *really knew* what they were doing? They'll recommend running one mile in the correct form rather than pushing to run two in a form that could hurt our body. Or they'd rather we do a 30-second plank properly than grind out a 60-second one with our back all jacked up in the wrong position. In other words, they want us to do less, but better.

Do less? This is something I can get behind. Our plates have a finite shape and capacity, and there just isn't space for 100 things on there at once anymore.

During our conversation, Pat and I decided we had to clearly define what was staying on our plate and what was coming off.

Here is what we came up with: If something doesn't directly impact our health, well-being, joy, and peace as individuals or as a family, it's off the plate. When we looked at our decisions, commitments, and tasks through this filter, it was quite easy (and freeing!)

to decide what stayed on and what came off. As a family, we could focus on less, better.

We may feel this way at school, too. I've had so many conversations with colleagues who are scrambling trying to do all the things they did in previous school years. But by keeping everything on our plates, we're doing far too much. We need to realign ourselves and give ourselves grace and permission to simplify our plate and focus on less.

With this year's group of students, we may not get to all 12 chapters in math—but we can do the first 11 well. Maybe this year, instead of students creating a big presentation where community members come in and act as judges, we'll scale it down and invite others from school to give feedback in the classroom.

How can we discern what stays on our plate and what comes off? By asking a few questions.

Is this directly impacting students and families? On the plate.

Did the sentence start with "Wouldn't it be cute if . . ."? Sounds like off-the-plate material at this time.

What stays on your plate? What comes off?

Give yourself permission to do less, better.

Small Shifts, Big Gifts

TEACH
HAPPIER

Commit to uncommitting! Think of *one thing* you can take
off your plate at work or at home (bonus points if it affects
both!). At the end of the week, see if this makes an impact on
your overall happiness.

Set a personal or professional goal for the week based on one small shift.

Weekly Win: At the end of the week, jot down one great thing that happened.

20

Good Enough Go

We've learned a bit about toxic positivity, but what about toxic productivity? Essentially, toxic productivity is an unhealthy desire to be productive at all times and at all costs—even when it's not expected of you.

Did you catch that last part? *Even when it's not expected of you.*

Oftentimes the expectations we put on *ourselves* make us frantically overproductive. Stressed. Weary. Have you ever felt like a failure just because you weren't *doing* something? I know I have. On nights and weekends, if I find myself not being productive, I can sometimes feel stressed . . . about *not being busy and stressed*. What in the world?! It's maddening!

Of course, it's admirable (and necessary!) to accomplish tasks at work or at home, but productivity becomes toxic when we are so hyperfocused on our tasks that we are in a constant state of frustration, overwhelm, and stress. According to a report in the *Harvard Business Review*, "The cognitive impact of feeling perpetually overwhelmed can range from mental slowness, forgetfulness, confusion, difficulty concentrating or thinking logically, to a racing mind or an impaired ability to problem solve" (Zucker, 2019). In other words, when our minds and bodies can't keep up with an overwhelmingly productive pace, and the complexity of our world surpasses the capacity of our mind, we can become physically or emotionally unhealthy. Thankfully, there are a few steps we can take to help us feel healthier and more aligned and balanced.

The first thing we need to do is recognize and acknowledge when we are in a state of overproductivity. Then, we need to discern our next right thing by reframing our thoughts. In an article about toxic productivity, author Brittany Wong (2021) suggests we eliminate the thought "What should I be doing right now?" and replace it with "What could I do, take care of, or create with ease now?" Furthermore, when our tired mind and body encourage us to do just *one more thing*, instead of hyperfocusing on what we haven't done, we should recall a few things that we have accomplished.

Another way we can reframe our thoughts is by applying a strategy I like to call "Good Enough Go." I learned this phrase from my husband years ago when I overheard him use it on a work call. Pat works for a big business in corporate America, so our jobs have almost nothing in common. (For the record, neither one of us would survive in the other person's job!)

"What in the world does 'good enough go' mean?" I asked.

He said, "After we've worked a long time on a project, there always comes a time when everyone starts getting into the weeds and starts paying attention to things that just won't make a difference, so someone has to call it 'good enough go.' The project may not be perfect, but it's ready. It's good enough to go."

My word. Is there a more fitting phrase? I can think of a thousand times at home or at school when I've found myself overthinking some detail that just. Doesn't. Matter. I need to get better at saying "good enough go."

Here are a few recent examples of times I've used this phrase at work or at home:

- I spent way too many minutes hemming and hawing over the color scheme of PowerPoint slides for a 6th grade model lesson. I kept asking myself, "Are greens or blues better this time of year?" Good grief! Pick a color and move along—*good enough go*.

- I tried to complete all my to-dos after school so I could check them all off my list. Spoiler alert: I couldn't accomplish them all. I could do three tasks. *Good enough go*.

- As I was helping my daughter with her homework, I noticed there were a few mistakes after spending about 25 minutes totally dialed in. My sanity won. *Good enough go.*

- I volunteered to bring something to my son's class party. I had all these ideas of bringing homemade baked goods or crafts. I didn't have that in me, so I signed up for cups and napkins. *Good enough go.*

The term "good enough go" isn't meant to be flippant or funny; it's meant for us to check our thoughts and energies and be sure we are putting them in the healthiest, most productive place. As educators, parents, partners, friends, siblings, and so much else, we're always going to have busy lives. There will always be endless tasks to complete. Try to lean in and listen to your mind, body, and spirit and notice when the focus on your checklists and to-dos becomes unsustainable. Choose what serves you, your family, and your students well. You have the option of healthy productivity or toxic productivity.

Small Shifts, Big Gifts

When you notice yourself becoming frustrated and over-whelmed with tasks at work or at home, ask yourself, "What can I do, take care of, or create with ease *now?*" and see if that helps you discern your next right thing.

If you've done all that is realistically possible, give yourself permission to feel OK that you've done what you can and declare, "Good enough go!"

Set a personal or professional goal for the week based on one small shift.

Weekly Win: At the end of the week, jot down one great thing that happened.

REPORT CARD

2

Yesterday I was clever, so I wanted to change the world.
Today I am wise, so I am changing myself.

— Rumi —

To paraphrase Bon Jovi, you're halfway there! Now it's time to take a breath, reflect on what you've learned these past few weeks, and direct your next small shifts in thoughts, language, and actions.

TAKEAWAYS

Review and summarize what was meaningful to you during the last 10 weeks.

11. Finding the Magic
12. What's Your Weekend Wish?
13. What Could Go *Right?*
14. December Is the New August
15. Grown-Ups Need to Have Fun
16. Plan Happier
17. Just Say No
18. *Even If . . .*
19. Do Less, Better
20. Good Enough Go

Reflections

Scan for the good! Review your Weekly Wins. What is something that makes you proud or especially happy? Are these Weekly Wins helping you tell the story you recorded in the "Before You Begin" chapter on page 7?

Name one or two small shifts you've incorporated in your personal or professional life that have made a positive impact at work and/ or at home. These may be shifts you want to incorporate long term. Can you articulate the impact of these small shifts in your life?

Name one or two small shifts you didn't have the bandwidth for earlier but want to practice soon. What do you hope to accomplish by incorporating these small shifts in your personal or professional life?

Look back to your original happiness baseline (see Figure i.1 on p. 6). Overall, are you feeling more content and aligned now? If so, describe how. If not, consider what small shifts in thoughts, language, or actions could help you feel an increase in your overall happiness at work or at home.

Where would you place yourself on the happiness continuum today? If possible, jot down a few reasons why.

MARKING PERIOD

3

" Most people need
consistency more
than they need
intensity. Intensity
makes a good story.
Consistency makes
progress. "

— James Clear —

21

Yes, Thank You

On the Teach Happier Facebook page, I encouraged people to share what toxic positivity means to them. Here are some of the responses I received:

- "Toxic positivity rejects real emotions."
- "It's condescending, dismissive, exhausting, annoying."
- "It makes me feel unseen."
- "Toxic positivity makes my experiences or feelings seem invalid."

Someone even said it was worse than toxic negativity! Why? Because when we are struggling and someone says, "Well, at least it isn't as bad as X," or "Look on the bright side," it can make us think that our feelings are invalid and wrong.

Does it seem weird to talk about toxic positivity in this space of positive psychology? It may, but this is something we need to be aware of as a community of rational optimists.

We've already learned that there is no such thing as work/life balance—it is not attainable or sustainable, since we are never truly 50/50, killing it at both work and home. It depends on the personal or professional season. For example, a good friend of mine is a leader in a neighboring school district and has been recently challenged by his school board for his work on diversity, equity, and inclusion. School board meetings are hostile and aggressive, and everything he does is being monitored by a group of community members. I would imagine right now he's probably 70 percent engaged at work and 30 at home. He's expending a great deal of energy trying to navigate these challenges at work and, sadly, that leaves little energy for his family when he gets home.

Can we acknowledge this is hard? Yep. Can we say this is tiring? You bet. Is it OK to admit this? YES. This is a heavy season for my friend. But he has shared with me something that has helped him, and I hope it can help you, too. He accepts help from those he trusts when it's offered.

Inner calm determines outer productivity, so when you're in a heavy season, it may be hard for you to be giving your all everywhere. As my friend struggles to complete tasks either personally or professionally, the last thing he needs is someone telling him, "It'll all be OK" or "You've got this" or the dreaded "Everything happens for a reason" (gah!). This kind of toxic positivity will not serve him; in fact, it will make things worse by invalidating his feelings.

One of the hallmarks of happy people is that they've developed strategies for coping and can access them when needed, which is what my friend is doing. Learning how to say yes when help is offered is one such strategy. But just as it can be hard to say no to somebody asking *for* help, it can also be hard to say yes when someone seeks *to* help. Think of the word *help* as an acronym:

- *H* stands for being *honest* with yourself and acknowledging when things are hard.

- *E* stands for *extending* yourself to someone you trust (not everyone gets the right to hear your vulnerable story!).

- *L* stands for *letting* others support you.

- *P* stands for *prioritizing* your peace.

If you are also in a season that is exhausting and overwhelming, consider saying yes when someone offers you help. As teachers and partners and parents and friends, we are often the helpers, the givers, the nurturers—and when we help, give to, and nurture others, we feel good. When things get hard for us, we need to give ourselves grace and accept help when it's offered. Because guess what? The person helping you will feel good about it, too.

Here's your invitation this week: If someone offers to listen to or help you in some way, don't default to "no, thank you," but rather lean into the offer.

Someone is willing to take the lead on [insert work obligation here]? *Yes, thank you.*

Someone offers to carpool your kid to practice so you can have a moment? *Yes, thank you.*

Someone suggests going on a walk together so you can get some of your thoughts out of your heart and into the world? *Yes, thank you.*

A colleague offers to copy or share lesson plans with you? *Yes, thank you.*

Don't feel like you have to rush to get *over* something in order to make other people comfortable. Take your time to go *through* it. As our wise friend Dr. Brené Brown (2015) reminds us in *Rising Strong,* "We don't have to do it alone. We were never meant to."

Some people see teachers as superheroes. We're not. In my opinion, that label is just another example of toxic positivity. Sure, we've been doing incredible work as we continue to navigate a postpandemic world, but we're not superheroes. We're *human beings.* And as human beings, we can find life hard or painful.

When the world feels too loud, it's OK to get quiet.

So get quiet and be honest with yourself, then use your voice to extend to others—and then let them help.

Small Shifts, Big Gifts

Right now, what is challenging in your life? Walk through the letters of the *HELP* acronym and resist the urge to do everything on your own. If someone you trust offers to hear you out or support you, lean into that offer with a "Yes, thank you" and see if that impacts your overall sense of peace and contentment.

Set a personal or professional goal for the week based on one small shift.

Weekly Win: At the end of the week, jot down one great thing that happened.

22

Tackle Teacher To-Dos

Just the other day, I was faced with a long list of tiny to-dos. You know what I'm talking about: emails to write, files to upload, plans to create, and a myriad of other mundane teacher tasks. It often seems like the minute I make my way through the list, I immediately find another sticky note and begin a new one. It can be maddening and overwhelming.

This week, I'll share a strategy for dealing with long to-do lists that has helped me for years. When faced with lots of little tasks, I prioritize how I will get them done by considering three things:

- **Tackle tasks that take one minute or less.** In *The Happiness Project* (2009a), Gretchen Rubin shares this brilliant idea: If a task will take you a minute or less to complete, do it as soon as you realize it needs to be done. That means if you see, say, "text Donna and Sarah about Thursday" or "sign permission slip," immediately do it the moment you see it on your list. Once I started applying this rule, those mundane to-dos were knocked right off in no time. Not only could I *see* things were getting done, I could *feel* that things were getting done!

- **Eat your frogs.** In *Eat That Frog! 21 Ways to Stop Procrastinating and Get More Done in Less Time* (2017), Brian Tracy refers to necessary but undesirable tasks as "frogs." My frog is usually a phone call, a workout, or an errand. When Tracy says to eat the frog, he means get it out of the way as early in the day as possible. It is proven that our days are happier and more efficient when we do this. Tracy says, "The more important the completed task, the happier, more confident and more powerful you feel about yourself and your world. . . . The completion of that important task triggers the release of endorphins in your brain, which can increase your confidence and creativity." He goes on to say, "Starting with your most difficult job, or piece of the job, gives you a jump start on the day. As a result, you'll be more energized and productive from then on . . . you will feel better about yourself, will personally feel more powerful, more effective, more in control and more in charge of your life" (p. 91).

I have found in my own experience that this works beautifully. For example, in my classroom, we sometimes disrupt our schedule to knock out an assessment early in the day. When I am doing office work, I try to complete difficult emails or phone calls first thing in order to free up my head and heart for the remaining tasks. And at home, my workout happens in the morning before heading to work, and dinner prep begins as soon as I get home from work. Eat that frog!

- **Free up your headspace and heartspace.** Maybe it's because I'm in my 40s, but I have recently become very protective of both my headspace and my heartspace. If something is really nagging at me, like a difficult conversation with someone or some big chore that I keep thinking about, I assess how much space it's taking up in my head or heart. If it's a lot—that is, if I keep thinking and thinking about it—then that's a cue that I need to get it over with as soon as possible to free up some headspace and heartspace. I have never regretted this method of decision making; it helps align my head and heart, which is my definition of peace.

When faced with a lot of personal or professional to-dos, see if these three strategies help you tackle them efficiently, with minimal annoyance and maximum satisfaction.

TEACH
HAPPIER

Small Shifts, Big Gifts

In what ways can you streamline your to-dos? Consider the three strategies shared and decide which you want to try this week.

Set a personal or professional goal for the week based on one small shift.

Weekly Win: At the end of the week, jot down one great thing that happened.

Objective: Students will proactively plan how they will accomplish short- or long-term tasks by applying the three strategies shared in this chapter.

Procedure
1. Read and summarize the chapter for students.
2. Have students create a three-column chart—one column per strategy.
3. Through a think-aloud, model a task in your personal or professional life that could be accomplished in one minute or less. As a class, brainstorm common tasks that could be accomplished in that time frame.
4. Have students jot down at least three things that they could do in one minute or less (either at school or at home).
5. Through a think-aloud, model an undesirable task in your personal or professional life that needs to be accomplished. Explain how you will "eat that frog" to get it done earlier in your day.
6. Have students jot down at least one "frog" at school or at home that they could "eat."
7. Through a think-aloud, model a task in your personal or professional life that is taking up considerable headspace or heartspace. Try to model something students can relate to (e.g., having a tough conversation with a friend or family member, taking the first few steps for a long-term project).
8. Have students jot down one thing that is taking up headspace or heartspace in their lives.
9. Throughout the week, ask students to reflect on this approach to tasks to see if it makes a positive impact in their lives at school or at home.

23

What's Next?

You've already learned a bit about training your brain to scan for the good so you can recognize what is going right in your life. This week, I'd like you to consider scanning for the good that *lies ahead* of you.

Having something to look forward to primes our brains for positivity by immediately enhancing our dopamine levels. In her 2020 article "The Psychological Benefits of Having Something to Look Forward To," Kelsey Borresen notes that looking forward to things makes us feel more optimistic about the future, can pleasantly distract us from undesired tasks, can motivate us when we want to give up, and adds meaning to our lives.

The other day, I was driving home from work and noticed that the closer I got to my house, the slower I was driving. Has that ever happened to you? After a busy day at work, I just wasn't ready for the busy night at home cooking, cleaning, and caring for my little family. I wanted to extend that feeling of peace and serenity that only my quiet car can give me.

So what did I do to make an instant shift in my perspective? I envisioned the *good* that lay ahead of me that evening—the thing I could look forward to amid the cooking, cleaning, and caring.

Get ready to be underwhelmed. That thing I looked forward to? Climbing into bed, turning on my electric blanket, and reading. Simple and unexciting, but something I genuinely looked forward to.

Since we've gotten to know one another well in these past few months, I feel comfortable sharing some of the short- *and* long-term things I generally look forward to—and I encourage you to do the same. Here they are, in no particular order:

- Planning our annual girls' trip with Donna and Sarah (we're 20 years in!).
- During football season, counting down the seconds to the next Buffalo Bills game.
- Watching an episode of *Real Housewives of* [insert any city]. (Don't judge!)
- Day trips to the beach in the summer.
- Enjoying a good dinner that's already prepped and ready.

You can do this at work, too. Here are some things my colleagues and I are currently looking forward to:

- "Fat Fridays"—crockpots, snacks, and desserts out at lunchtime on the last Friday of the month. It's heavenly!
- An upcoming half-day for students that we can use to catch up on work.
- A beloved colleague returning from maternity leave.
- An outdoor happy hour once the weather gets a little nicer.

Some of these will happen today, and others will happen months from now. That doesn't matter. What's important is that I have trained myself to *access* these short- and long-term future moments to increase my happiness in the present.

Your invitation this week is to come up with a short list of moments that you are looking forward to that you can recall when you need to. The more moments you think about, the easier this practice is.

Want to boost your happiness *now?* Think about something good that will happen *next.*

TEACH HAPPIER

Small Shifts, Big Gifts

Make a list of things you can look forward to, either in the short or in the long term. Make it a priority to access this list when you are feeling frustrated, bored, unmotivated, or overwhelmed and see if it positively impacts your level of happiness.

Set a personal or professional goal for the week based on one small shift.

Weekly Win: At the end of the week, jot down one great thing that happened.

24

'Tis the Season

I don't especially love March. Up here in the northern United States, the skies are still gray, the snow is dirty and slushy and inconsistent, and we all just want spring to make its appearance.

But there is *one* thing I love about the month of March: Shamrock Shakes.

I love a McDonald's Shamrock Shake, and I won't apologize for it. These are a few things I look forward to each season, all food- or drink-related: Shamrock Shakes, pumpkin spice lattes, Girl Scout cookies, Rita's Italian Ice, Sam Adams Summer Ale.

I'm reminded of the time our friend Chad came to visit my husband and me after we'd had our first child. His kids were a little older, so he had some perspective to share (especially having two sets of twins!).

"Here's some advice," Chad said. "Try to enjoy every moment. Because everything from here on out is a season. So if it's hard, know that it will pass eventually. And if it's good, savor it, because it won't last forever."

When I think about it, that was the best advice I could have gotten as a new parent. Chad shared this wisdom when our daughter was one day old. Now my kids are young teenagers, and I think of that piece of advice almost every day. I was so grateful when the season of sleepless nights was over, yet it breaks my heart to think of the short season when my son would fly his Buzz Lightyear figure around in the backyard, lost in his make-believe world. Today, he's immersed in competitive basketball games. These are also the days of teenage moods and attitudes. Those of you who have been through these years know that understanding these days as a *season* is vital if you want to stay sane.

Again, it's about being a rational optimist: Rationally, we recognize that things continue to be challenging, exhausting, confusing, and just plain hard, but optimistically, we recognize that just about everything in this life is temporary. When it's good, we should savor it. When it's hard, we should rest assured it will eventually pass. Either way, we will continue to grow and move on.

This school year may seem *l-o-n-g*. Some days, it may feel like it will never end. But eventually it will. If you can appreciate where you are in this journey, even if it's not exactly where you want to be *yet*, you'll learn that every season serves a purpose before the next.

Your invitation this week is to reground yourself by recognizing and accepting that you are in a season, and like any season, it has a definite beginning and end. You're getting there.

One way to do this is by adding the words *right now* to any negative feelings you may be having. Give it a try:

- I am frustrated *right now*.

- I am really sad *right now*.

- I am overwhelmed *right now*.

Do you see the shift? When you add *right now*, you are acknowledging that the discomfort you feel is temporary. Better times are coming.

Now switch gears. What if you try adding *right now* to your positive feelings?

- I am joyful *right now*.

- I am so excited *right now*.

- I am grateful *right now*.

When you add *right now* to the positive feelings, you are emphasizing the moment. This can help you to really lean into and appreciate it.

Whether you are sad, happy, or something in between, by adding *right now* to your feelings, you can zoom out of your emotions to see the bigger picture.

All you have is time. All you have is *right now*.

TEACH HAPPIER

Small Shifts, Big Gifts

Think about the season you are currently in personally or professionally. What is going well? What is challenging? Consider making a small shift by adding *right now* to your feelings to reinforce the idea that you are in a *season*.

Set a personal or professional goal for the week based on one small shift.

Weekly Win: At the end of the week, jot down one great thing that happened.

25

Align Your Stars

This week I want to share two quick stories: one that happened three years ago and one that happened three weeks ago. Both are great examples of how we can help our stars align.

I'll start with the story from three weeks ago. I was talking with a very good friend and colleague who was thinking about her next right professional thing. "Maybe the stars will align and it will happen," she said.

I immediately responded: "SO ALIGN YOUR STARS!"

I didn't want my talented and amazing teacher friend to wait for the universe to magically align the stars so she could do her thing. Instead, we talked about how *she* could align her stars—people she could talk to, things she could look into, ideas she might develop and organize a bit more. I am happy to report that she is getting closer to the stars aligning.

Now let's go back three years, to the Teach Better Conference in Akron, Ohio. In November 2019, I was talking with Adam Welcome, an author, speaker, and all-around good guy. It's always been my dream to write a book, and I shared that with Adam.

"Maybe a book is your final destination, but maybe it isn't," he said. "I think you need to start a podcast. Give me your phone." And just like that, he downloaded the Anchor app and showed me how to use it.

The stars began to align.

Then he said, "I'm checking in on you in a month. You're doing this. What do you have to lose? If it's great, then awesome. And if nobody listens, you've lost nothing!"

Dear readers, I did not start that podcast within a month. Being in that sandwich generation of caring for aging parents and young children, I just didn't feel like it was the right time for a creative endeavor. Alas, my stars didn't align.

One month later, right on schedule, Adam called and asked, "When does the first episode drop?"

"I don't know, Adam," I said. "I'm not sure podcasting is in my wheelhouse."

"Suzanne Dailey, you are doing this," he said. He seemed so certain in his advice, I started to believe I could actually make a podcast.

So I did.

After that initial nudge, I decided to align my own stars.

And look what's happened.

As I write this, the *Teach Happier* podcast just celebrated its 75th episode. Because of the podcast, I've been able to connect with people all over the world and ultimately reach my dream of publishing the very book you are holding in your hands.

Your invitation this week is to look at your personal or professional life and ask yourself what could help you feel more aligned, content, balanced, fulfilled, proud, or *alive*. Is it time to consider changing grade levels or schools? Are you ready to explore another position in your district? Do you want to lean into coaching or running an extracurricular group? Do you need time and space and think a sabbatical may be the right thing in this season?

Don't wait for the stars to align. Go out and align them yourself.

TEACH HAPPIER

Small Shifts, Big Gifts

What could you proactively do to align your stars so you can meet a personal or professional goal?

Set a personal or professional goal for the week based on one small shift.

Weekly Win: At the end of the week, jot down one great thing that happened.

26

Find the Good Old Days Today

What would you consider "the good old days"—a season in your life that you look back on with happiness and gratitude? Maybe it's a moment in your childhood, or a college memory, or the day you held your newborn child. No matter your age, you can probably look back at a season or moment in your life and smile, recognizing that "those were the days."

Nostalgia can be a wonderful thing. By telling us good things have happened to us in the past, it primes us to understand that good things can happen in the future. But what about the present?

When you think back to some positive times, do you recall if you were able to recognize *at the time* that they'd be as sacred and meaningful to you as they are today? We often don't feel that way in the moment. For example, one happy memory I have from my childhood is of walking around my backyard. I had a beautiful backyard growing up in western New York, with the gift of the most magnificent autumns. I spent happy, serene moments walking around the acres and acres of the apple orchard behind my house in the fall, when the apples were so heavy they would bend the branches to the ground. Doesn't that sound so beautifully sacred? Although I would do anything *now* to go back, I am sure that in that moment, I was probably longing for more freedom and dreaming of the world beyond that backyard.

The happy, nostalgic snapshot of college? That would be hanging out with Donna, Sarah, and Colleen in O'Shea Hall at Niagara

University, eating chicken-finger subs and laughing our heads off at something ridiculous as we coordinated our Express outfits before going out to some dance club. I may have been laughing, but I can almost guarantee you that in the moment, I was feeling worried about some upcoming exam or assignment.

And those precious moments of holding my newborn son or daughter? I could weep right now just thinking of that sacred, nostalgic, tender time. Yet in that moment, I was more than likely exhausted and overwhelmed by the prospect of caring for the help-less little being. Now that I am in my 40s, I can tell you without hesi-tation that those were the good old days. But in that exact moment, when it was actually happening? Probably not.

Recently, I thought about this notion of recognizing the good old days in the present during a routine workday. A small group of us at school often work together to create, plan, and implement ideas for teachers and kids. It's hard work, but we invest in each other both in and out of work in very intentional ways. This makes us productive coworkers and genuine friends. A few days ago, we were collabo-rating and researching and planning and creating and laughing. We stopped what we were doing, looked around, and acknowledged the fact that right in that very moment *we were in the good old days.* Right *now.* We said it out loud, recognizing that one day we were going to look back with blissful nostalgia and reflect on this time with gratitude and happiness.

This made us stop. And smile. A few of us got teary (yes, I was one of them).

We need to start paying attention to the good stuff. One way I do this uses an idea from Emily P. Freeman's *The Next Right Thing Guided Journal* (2021b). Every month, I fill in a blank chart labeled "These are the days of . . ." with things like the following:

- Spending time at the barn with my daughter.

- Sitting on the porch with Pat and a cup of coffee on a sunny weekend.

- Talking with Brian as we try to figure out how to do life without Mom and support Dad as he does the same.

- Laughing with Jason about some inside work joke.

- Hearing a basketball dribble on our hardwood floors.

- Talking and connecting with Dad like never before.

- Making hard decisions for our child in an effort to support a variety of needs.

- Returning flexible seating to classrooms.

- Moving forward with work projects under changing leadership.

- Transitioning from winter sports to spring sports.

- Supporting friends and family with scary diagnoses.

- Calling to catch up with the matriarch of our family, my beloved Nan.

There are a lot of happy things on this list, but it also captures the challenging things. After all, I know I will look back on these lists with happiness and gratitude one day and say, "Those were the good old days."

Your invitation this week is to take a little inventory of your life *right now*. Honor something that's good about *today*. Scan for something in your personal or professional life that will one day have you looking back fondly and with gratitude. Something that will make you stop, smile, and maybe even get a little teary.

Find tomorrow's good old days today.

Small Shifts, Big Gifts

TEACH HAPPIER

As you examine this current season in your life, think about what makes them the good old days. Either scan for the good or try to make a list like the one I made and see if it adjusts your perspective to reveal what's special about this current time in your life.

Set a personal or professional goal for the week based on one small shift.

Weekly Win: At the end of the week, jot down one great thing that happened.

27

Extravagant Kindness

Fill in the blank: "_____ acts of kindness."

Did you say *random?* I thought you might. That's what I used to think, too. When you think of a random act of kindness, you may think about paying for coffee for the person behind you or leaving a little anonymous note in somebody's mailbox or holding the door open for someone.

However, positive psychologists invite us to shift from random acts of kindness to *conscious* acts of kindness. After all, when you think of the prepaid coffee, anonymous note, or door-holding gesture, none of them is really random; they're very intentional, deliberate acts to put some positivity into the world.

According to positive psychologists, the fastest way to increase your short-term happiness is by performing a conscious act of kindness, which promotes actual physiological changes in the brain. In an article titled "Why Science Says Helping Others Makes Us Happier" (2018), author Maria Baltazzi writes that, just as runners can get a "runner's high" from running, "you can experience a similar feeling without busting a lung when you give someone a hand. Though instead it is called *Helper's High*—a euphoria that happens when you do charitable deeds. The psychological theory being that giving, acts of kindness, produce a natural mild version of a morphine high" (para. 6).

Furthermore, behavioral health counselor Steve Siegle (2020) claims that "[p]hysiologically, kindness can positively change your brain. Being kind boosts serotonin and dopamine, which are neu-rotransmitters in the brain that give you feelings of satisfaction and well-being, and cause the pleasure/reward centers in your brain to light up" (para. 3).

When we need to lift our spirits, the best thing we can do is lift someone *else* up. Moving from random to conscious acts of kindness reminds us that this is within our thoughtful control. *We get to decide when we want to extend kindness and compassion toward others.*

These months of the school year are typically busy and stressful. It's easy to feel like the list of things to get done is out of your control, but you *do* have control over finding opportunities to strengthen personal and professional relationships through conscious acts of kindness.

A few days ago, I decided I would perform some conscious act of kindness in any school I visited. This became my "happiness mission"—doing what I could to lift others up. These were not grand, sweeping gestures. I sent a simple text to at least three colleagues per school to let them know I was thinking about them; I emailed a colleague to thank them for going the extra mile for a school event that brought the community together; I delivered a hot cup of coffee (and one Red Bull) to the new teachers in the hallway. The best thing about these conscious acts of kindness is that they're a win-win: Not only do they lift others up, but they increase your own happiness, too.

My district promotes conscious acts of kindness by encouraging us to use our interoffice mail to "Kind" someone. It's kind of like get-ting "Boo'd" at Halloween, but instead you get "Kinded." Happiness is literally circling our district! It is so fun to receive one of these envelopes, but it feels even better to thank the colleague who sent it. These small acts nurture relationships among 1,500 colleagues, directly impacting the climate of our buildings and classrooms.

To remain consistent about conscious acts of kindness, I set a cal-endar reminder a couple of days a week to reach out and strengthen my connection with a friend, family member, neighbor, or colleague.

Sometimes I add it to my task-reminder app—then I get to perform an act of kindness *and* cross something off a list!

As you share your gratitude with others, also remember that *humble voices travel farther*. The ultimate goal is to be others-oriented by performing the conscious act of kindness and not telling anyone about it!

Here's to elevating random acts of kindness to conscious acts of kindness—an extravagant 2-degree shift.

TEACH
HAPPIER

Small Shifts, Big Gifts

Think of at least one person in your personal and professional life and plan to share a conscious act of kindness with them. See what that conscious act of kindness does for your happiness baseline!

Set a personal or professional goal for the week based on one small shift.

Weekly Win: At the end of the week, jot down one great thing that happened.

Objective: Students will proactively plan to perform a conscious act of kindness at school or at home and reflect on its impact.

Procedure

1. Summarize the chapter for students.
2. As a class, choose an adult in the building (custodian, lunch staff, office staff) who makes a positive impact on your school's climate.
3. Together, brainstorm some conscious acts of kindness you could perform for that person (bonus points if you carry through with this plan!).
4. Have students choose someone at home or school and think of a conscious act of kindness that would increase someone else's happiness.
5. Ask students to notice whether their levels of happiness are increasing as they imagine this conscious act of kindness.
6. If possible, share and reflect as students complete their conscious acts of kindness. Some teachers like to have a place in the room (like a graffiti board) where students can write what they did and how they feel. It's a great way to keep the conversation going!

28

Vacation Mode . . . Today!

"Many of us are not practicing self-care, we are practicing *after* care," writes Nedra Tawwab in *Set Boundaries, Find Peace* (2021). "After care is what we do once we are diminished and depleted. Self-care is preventative. It is used to stay well and maintain your peace." This hit home for me, and I imagine it does for many of you, too.

To unpack this idea a little more, let me introduce you to someone my family lovingly calls "Vacation Suzanne." You see her only a few times of the year, during an extended school break, and let me tell you, she is a good time. She's not up at 5 a.m. to work out. She's not planning or cooking meals. She's not driving from building to building to teach, consult, meet, and problem solve. Errands? No, ma'am. Cleaning? No, sir.

Vacation Suzanne is *s-l-o-w*. She doesn't want to lead. Or make a decision. Or plan. Or do much of anything but just *be*.

It's been a family joke for years, and we laugh about it, but I recently realized that Vacation Suzanne represents what Tawwab was referring to: after care.

Work Suzanne thinks, "After I finish the plans for the 6th grade writing club, I'll indulge in an old episode of *Parks and Recreation*." "After I push myself for a five-mile run, I'll collapse and enjoy the banana bread we made yesterday." "After I clear out some of these emails, I can call Nichole to catch up."

Do you see why it's called *after* care? Because it's what I do only after taking care of responsibilities. Like Tawwab says, I feel diminished and depleted. When I feel this way, I can easily check out. Mindlessly scroll. Fall asleep watching a show.

This has made me realize the need to stop and care for myself *preventatively*. I recognize I don't need to wait until I'm ready to fall apart to care for myself. I have to catch myself and care for myself now, in the present moment.

"As a preventative measure, we need to lean into continuous and consistent self-care practices," says Tawwab. In other words, we can't treat our minds and bodies the way some people treat their cars, ignoring the engine light until the problem becomes "real."

This week's invitation is to try and engage in continuous, present-moment self-care. Vacation You needs to merge with Work You. Find ways to care for yourself *while* undertaking tasks rather than wait until afterward, when you're too weary. This will help you show up better for your family, your colleagues, and yourself.

TEACH HAPPIER

Small Shifts, Big Gifts

What do you practice more often: continuous, consistent self-care, or after care? If it's self-care, good for you! What are the conditions or boundaries you have in your life to promote and support this? If you notice you practice after care more often, what are some conditions or boundaries you can put in place to help make self-care more continuous and consistent in your life?

Set a personal or professional goal for the week based on one small shift.

Weekly Win: At the end of the week, jot down one great thing that happened.

29

Who Are Your People?

Most of our success after the age of 21 is almost *entirely interdependent on others*. Think about that for a moment. Are you successful only because of *your* actions? Certainly not. Much of it has to do with who you choose to surround yourself with, both personally and professionally.

According to research (Feeney & Collins, 2014), there is a link between strong relationships and success. Feeney and Collins observe that a thriving life can be attained by having a strong support system. Our connections and relationships give us the space to talk through ideas, troubleshoot, share resources, and connect to new people.

In *Braving the Wilderness*, Brené Brown (2017) talks about how, prior to the invention of the household washing machine, women would gather by the river to wash their clothes communally, talking, complaining, problem solving, and supporting one another. Once the washing machine was invented, they were suddenly alone in their homes while completing this task, and they missed the socialization and presence of community.

More recently, according to Shawn Achor (2018), there has been an all-time high demand for single dorm rooms in U.S. colleges. Why? Because many students are worried that other people will be a distraction to their success. But when positive psychologists study our most successful, resilient, happy people, they find that the *one* thing they all have in common is a set of strong social relationships with a diverse and inclusive group of people.

A fascinating social psychology study (Schnall et al., 2008) asked people to stand alone at the bottom of a hill and predict its incline. Later, those same participants were asked to look at the same exact hill, but this time alongside somebody they trusted. Guess what? That hill now looked 10 to 20 percent less steep!

If you want to be as happy and successful as possible, you need to prioritize nurturing healthy relationships: the ones that don't get in the way of our tasks and accomplishments, but rather give us energy, perspective, and support.

Who are your people? Shawn Achor would ask that you think about those who leave you feeling good, who strengthen you, and who make you hope for more. Anyone who does all three of those things is one of your people. (Figure 29.1 is based on Achor's idea of creating a Venn diagram of these three criteria.)

In her book *Wolfpack*, U.S. soccer legend Abby Wambach explains her philosophy of "point and run." If you watch any videos of her playing, you will notice that when she scores a goal, she starts pointing. She'll point to the person who assisted the goal, to the coach who called the play, to the teammate who defended another player to give her space to do her thing. In other words, when she succeeds, she honors those around her who supported that success.

It's time to nurture relationships by showing some gratitude to your people.

Start pointing.

Small Shifts, Big Gifts

Move through this week in a space of gratitude! Complete the Venn diagram in Figure 29.1 to figure out who your people are. Each day this week, write one thank-you note or a send a quick text to let someone know how much you appreciate their contributions (think custodial staff, instructional support staff, secretaries, cafeteria staff, etc.). See if doing this increases your levels of happiness.

Figure 29.1 Who Are Your People?

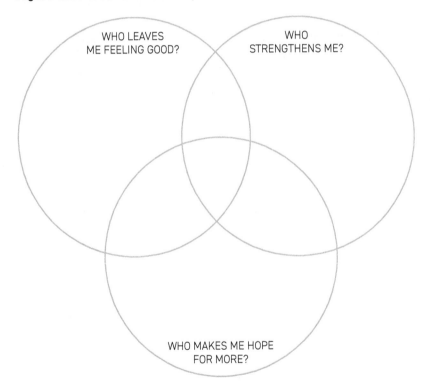

Set a personal or professional goal for the week based on one small shift.

Weekly Win: At the end of the week, jot down one great thing that happened.

Objective: Students will show gratitude to someone in their lives who strengthens them.

Procedure

1. Read or summarize this chapter for students.
2. Draw a Venn diagram on the board and label it like the one in Figure 29.1.
3. Through a think-aloud, model celebrating one or two people who strengthen you, make you hope for more, and leave you feeling good.
4. Ask students to think about someone in their lives who meets these same three criteria for them. (Note: You may want to explicitly say it can't be you, as they may all use you as the example. As sweet as that is, you want them to think about others in their lives.)
5. Give students time to share their person with the class.
6. Hand out thank-you notes. Give students 10 minutes to write a letter of gratitude to their chosen person.
7. Over the next couple of weeks, ask students if they've received a response from the person they wrote to. This is a teachable moment to celebrate the fact that when we make someone else feel good, our levels of happiness go up as well. Conscious act of kindness plus gratitude plus strengthening relationships equals exponential happiness!

30

Keep Your Eyes on Your Own Paper

This weekend I went for a run. It's one of the things that keeps me physically and mentally strong. It was a beautiful, somewhat foggy morning. There were birds singing, Foo Fighters blaring in my ear-buds, and forsythia blooming. I felt strong. And energized. And fast.

And then a little voice interrupted the music to announce my time for my first mile. Turns out I was, well, *slow*. Like, a *lot* slower than I wanted to be. I was disappointed. "Come on, Suzanne," I scolded myself, "you can do better! You can run faster! What is going on today?"

And then I thought: These are *my* miles today. This is *my* run. This is *my* pace. I quit comparing the way I was running with how I ran before and acknowledged what I was accomplishing *right now*.

And then I kept running.

This week, I'd like you to take a little advice that you may have given students at one time or another: *Keep your eyes on your own paper.*

I don't know about you, but I see my colleagues doing *amazing* things, both at school and on social media. Some are transforming their classrooms into different worlds. Others are Bitmoji-ing the heck out of their directions and classroom decorations. Still others are sending personalized Pinterest-perfect packages to students and families during the holidays. It's incredible. But these amazing things *others* are doing can make *me* feel a bit inadequate.

And that's why I've got to keep my eyes on my own paper.

Your best is good enough. It's more than good enough—it's downright incredible.

Positive psychologists claim that social comparison is normal behavior and can be useful in helping us determine if we're on track. However, in an article for PositivePsychology.com, Dr. Alicia Nortje (2020) states that comparing ourselves with others against an unrealistic benchmark can be "extremely harmful and result in negative thoughts and behaviors" (para. 2).

Are you great with technology and rocking interactive lessons with all the bells and whistles? Awesome.

Are your students growing as readers and writers with simple books and journals? Phenomenal.

Do you have a personalized greeting for each one of your students? Amazing.

Are you quietly checking in on a few students who need to know they are loved? Spectacular.

Do you email one family every day to give a child a compliment? Outstanding.

Is an extended recess on a sunny day going to help your wellness? Fantastic.

I couldn't keep up my regular pace during this morning's run, and that's OK. It doesn't make me a bad runner. And we can't always keep up our pace with everybody else, and *that's* OK, too. This doesn't make us bad teachers. Many of us are balancing multiple roles right now, and I am certain that we are all doing the very best we can. But if we constantly compare ourselves with others, we will never see that our best is good enough.

Find a pace you can maintain. Some days you'll be moving faster or slower than other days, and that's OK.

And remember to keep your eyes on your own paper.

Small Shifts, Big Gifts

TEACH
HAPPIER

Keep your eyes on your own paper as you scan for the good and scan for the wins! Each day this week, acknowledge something you have done to help your home family, your classroom family, or yourself to grow. Remember, these do not have to be revolutionary shifts—just things that helped move things in a positive direction. When we train our brains to look for the wins *on our own paper*, we increase the likelihood of doing more good things in the future.

Set a personal or professional goal for the week based on one small shift.

Weekly Win: At the end of the week, jot down one great thing that happened.

3

The more reflective you are, the more effective you are.

— Pete Hall and Alisa Simeral —

You've made it to Week 30! *30!* You are rounding the corner to the final stretch of the school year. It's now time to reflect on what you've learned these past few weeks and direct your next small shifts in thoughts, language, and actions.

Review and summarize what was meaningful to you during the last 10 weeks.

21. Yes, Thank You
22. Tackle Teacher To-Dos
23. What's Next?
24. 'Tis the Season
25. Align Your Stars
26. Find the Good Old Days Today
27. Extravagant Kindness
28. Vacation Mode . . . Today!
29. Who Are Your People?
30. Keep Your Eyes on Your Own Paper

Reflections

Scan for the good! Review your Weekly Wins. What is something that makes you proud or especially happy? Are these Weekly Wins helping you tell the story you recorded in the "Before You Begin" chapter on page 7?

Name one or two small shifts you've incorporated in your personal or professional life that have made a positive impact at work and/ or at home. These may be shifts you want to incorporate long term. Can you articulate the impact of these small shifts in your life?

Name one or two small shifts you didn't have the bandwidth for earlier but want to practice soon. What do you hope to accomplish by incorporating these small shifts in your personal or professional life?

Look back to your original happiness baseline (see Figure i.1 on p. 6). Overall, are you feeling more content and aligned now? If so, describe how. If not, consider what small shifts in thoughts, language, or actions could help you feel an increase in your overall happiness at work or at home.

Where would you place yourself on the happiness continuum today? If possible, jot down a few reasons why.

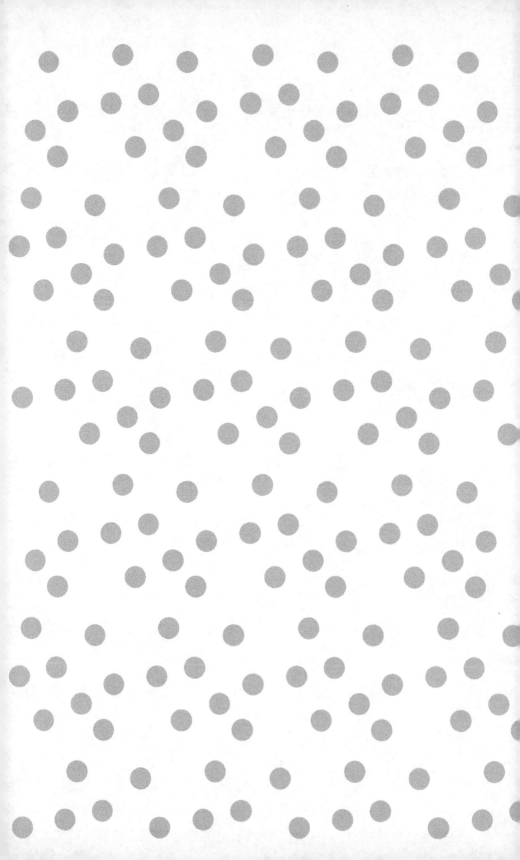

" **The fourth quarter is ours.** "

— Coach Buck Nystrom —

31

The Fourth Quarter Is Yours

If we want to feel happier, we have to be disciplined about prioritizing practices that are based in positive psychology. Remember, it's not what we do every once in a while that makes a difference but, rather, small, incremental shifts applied frequently that make an impact over time.

There are some points in the school year when this kind of discipline is especially necessary, and this is one of those times. You are in the final stretch—managing parent conferences, report cards, and transition meetings; assessing what's left to teach before the end of the year; and preparing for traditional end-of-year traditions and celebrations. It's bananas.

You can see the finish line ahead if you squint, but it's still quite a distance away. You know you're going to need to muster up some of that optimism and energy from the beginning of the school year to make it. And you know what can help you accomplish this? College football.

Did you know that some college football teams hold up four fingers at the beginning of the fourth quarter? This has been traced back to legendary college football coach Buck Nystrom. When teams hold up four fingers as the final quarter begins, they are signaling "The fourth quarter is ours." No matter the score, it's a reminder that players must remain all in and play their hearts out until the final whistle. You can tell where this is headed, right?

As a teacher, how do you enter the fourth quarter of the school year with a disciplined happiness? The answer should be familiar by now: Scan for what is going right for you this school year. Locate the wins, both big and small.

It can be a challenge at this time of the school year to look around at *everyone else's* students, classrooms, and overall achievement and notice your deficits by comparison:

- Look how organized her classroom still is. Mine is a wreck!

- I can't believe my students' test scores aren't as high as his students'.

- How are they possibly on Unit 10 when we just got through with 8?

In this last quarter, it's easy to become hyperfocused on our perceived shortcomings. But positive psychology invites us to scan for the strengths when we want to default to our perceived weaknesses. So look around at *your* students, classroom, and overall achievement and notice the *wins*:

- What child began this school year with anxiety and can now walk into the classroom ready to learn? High five.

- Which student told you in October that he'll "never read unless my teacher tells me to" and now can't put down a series you introduced him to? Fist bump.

- And how about that parent who questioned your "crazy, unstructured classroom with yoga balls, standing desks, and pillows" and is now thanking you? Big hugs all around.

Here's the thing: Kids don't do as we say; they do as *they see*. Kids will remember how we finish this school year.

Oprah Winfrey (2017) has a sign in her meeting room. It says, "You are responsible for the energy you bring into this space." So scan for the wins, strengthen your relationships, and end this unique year strong, no matter the score.

You are entering the fourth quarter. This is it. Rekindle the optimism and enthusiasm you had in your first week to round out the year.

The fourth quarter is yours.

TEACH
HAPPIER

Small Shifts, Big Gifts

How do you want your students to remember this year
with you? You may want to revisit your goals from the very
beginning of the book to recapture some of your earlier
thoughts. Envision *one* proactive thing you can do this week
to help meet those goals.

Set a personal or professional goal for the week based on one small shift.

Weekly Win: At the end of the week, jot down one great thing that happened.

Objective: Students will proactively plan ways to remain present and all in for the remainder of the school year!

Procedure
1. Read or summarize this chapter for students.
2. Through a think-aloud, share how teachers get tired and over-whelmed at the end of the year and need to make the decision to act the way they want to feel, but this takes work!
3. Model a few ways you will adjust your thoughts, actions, or language to approach the last quarter of the school year with energy and optimism.
4. Ask students to write down at least two ways they will adjust their thoughts, actions, or language to approach the school year with energy and enthusiasm. (Some classrooms have made this a bulletin board that is overtly displayed for the rest of the year. When a teacher or classmate recognizes someone doing some-thing from the bulletin board, this can be celebrated together!)

32

Extreme Phone Makeover

Do you have a love/hate relationship with your phone? It helps you stay connected to others, but sometimes it drives you crazy: the screen randomly lighting up, the unexpected buzzing, the endless notifications for your kids' school—it's just all too much sometimes. With that in mind, here are some small, proactive shifts you can make in your relationship to your phone that will help you gain peace, contentment, and alignment.

Adjust Your Notification Settings

The other day I was in a meeting, and my colleague kept picking up her phone to check it whenever it vibrated or the screen lit up—again and again and again. We've grown conditioned to constantly checking our phones. It's almost like we need to tell our phones they are not the boss of us.

Red notification circles, we're looking at you. We don't like seeing you constantly pop up in the right-hand corner of our apps. Same goes for you, beeps, banners, and alerts. You tear us away from what we're doing or thinking multiple times a day.

I mean, do we really care if Ann Taylor Loft is having *another* sale? Is it crucial that to know that our colleague started a Voxer account and is now Voxing at this very moment in time? Will it change the course of our day to know that Facebook proclaims it's National Pancake Day?

If you answered no to any of these, it's time to adjust those notification settings. By doing this, you are literally silencing the noise around you, allowing you to concentrate on what matters.

Simplify Your Inbox

People tend to fall into one of two groups: those who delete email messages or move them to folders upon reading (bless us, each and every one), and those who let thousands of emails pile up in their inbox (savages!).

One way to decrease the amount of noise coming at you is to organize your personal email account by unsubscribing from mailing lists that no longer serve you. At the beginning of each year, at least once a day, I unsubscribe from an automated mailing list I put myself on years ago to get a 15-percent-off coupon code. Pressing that "Unsubscribe" button feels so freeing, and when I see fewer emails piling up each day, I feel a greater sense of peace and order.

Use Your Timer

Ever find yourself thinking, "I'm just going to get back to a few people on email and call it a day" or "Let me just do a quick scroll and see what's happening on Instagram" and then realize you've been sucked in for 90 minutes? It's the worst. You feel totally sapped. Shawn Achor attributes this to too much passive leisure time. In a blog post titled "There's a Reason Why Your Free Time Is So Draining" (2021), he shares that research shows activities such as watching TV and scrolling on social media are enjoyable and engaging for only about 30 minutes before they start sapping our energy, creating what psychologists call "psychic entropy"—a feeling of listlessness and apathy.

To conserve my limited amounts of mental energy, I've started setting my phone timer. At nighttime, if I want to see what's happening on social media, I will set a timer for 15 minutes, get my scroll on, and then get out of there when I hear the chime.

When my timer goes off a few minutes before I have to leave at the end of the workday, I know I need to finish up what I'm working on and prepare myself to switch gears and start thinking about home.

Move Your Social Media

This may not be a popular idea, but it's been a game changer for me. Every summer, I go on a "Facebook fast." I delete the app from my phone on the last day of school, and I merrily squeeze out extra summer minutes because, rather than looking at everyone else's summer, I'm enjoying my own. What's more, this year, when I ended my fast with the obligatory posts of my children on their first day of school, that little blue icon didn't get a premier spot on the front page of my phone. Nope—that icon moved right on back to the very last page. This has forced me to decide with every swipe—once, twice, three times—whether social media is how I want to spend my time and energy. And I'll tell you what: There are plenty of times when I think on the first or second swipe, "Not today, Facebook. Not today."

Game. Changer.

Airplane Mode or Bust

If you aren't careful, your workday can creep well into the night as you keep answering incoming emails or texts. To address this, my wise friend and colleague Kate (@KateCarrollCB) recommends putting your phone on airplane mode at a certain time and calling it a day.

My airplane mode time? Nine p.m. Every night. Hard stop. Texts and work email notifications may roll in, but airplane mode allows me to disconnect and rest so I can show up the next day with a whole new batch of patience, humor, grace, and kindness. Keep in mind, your own airplane mode time might be earlier!

Professional responsibilities can feel overwhelming and out of our control. But these small actions are all within our control, and they can bring us greater peace, contentment, and alignment. I don't know about you, but that sure sounds like happiness to me.

TEACH HAPPIER

Small Shifts, Big Gifts

Are you up for giving your phone a bit of a makeover? Choose a few of the ideas in this chapter to implement and see if they make a positive difference!

Set a personal or professional goal for the week based on one small shift.

Weekly Win: At the end of the week, jot down one great thing that happened.

33

Rest Happier

Here you are in the final weeks of school, and you're probably tired—teacher tired. It can feel like hitting a wall.

I recently saw this post on Twitter by writer and actor Brandon Kyle Goodman (@brandonkgood): "I told my friend I was emotionally hitting a wall. Her response was, 'Sometimes walls are there so we can lean on them and rest.'"

Have you ever woken up after a good night's sleep and still felt exhausted? Me, too. But what if that level of exhaustion wasn't due to the quality of your sleep? What if it was due to a *rest deficit?* Many educators would say that the term *rest deficit* perfectly summarizes how they feel at this point in the school year.

As you anticipate a much-needed and well-deserved summer break, lean into the idea of rest—*real* rest. According to Saundra Dalton-Smith, author of *Sacred Rest* (2017), there are seven types of rest: physical, mental, emotional, social, creative, spiritual, and sensory. Understanding them can help us identify what our minds, bodies, and spirits need to feel rested and restored.

To Dalton-Smith, rest should be synonymous with restorative activities. In her article "The 7 Types of Rest That Every Person Needs," she says, "Sleep and rest are not the same thing. . . . We go through life thinking we've rested because we've gotten enough sleep—but in reality we are missing out on the other types of rest we desperately need" (2021, paras. 2, 3).

Each type of rest is explained below. As you read about them, consider the two that you need the most and one you would like to consider creating space for. This will help prioritize allotting time and space to activities that help us feel restored and genuinely rested.

On the Teach Happier Facebook page, I asked our members what they did to feel rested and rejuvenated. The percentages below reflect the breakdown of answers. Note that there is a physical move representing each type of rest at the end of each explanation; these are the moves I use when I teach students about this concept.

Creative Rest (43 percent)

If you're having trouble thinking of new ideas or solving a problem, you could use some creative rest. Activities like reading, writing, spending time in nature, drawing, painting, and cooking are examples of creative rest. (*Physical move*: Pretend to draw or paint.)

Physical Rest (24 percent)

This is what most of us think about when we consider rest. There is *passive* rest like napping or lounging, and then there is *active* rest like stretching, walking, or yoga. Both active and passive rest help us feel restored and energized. We know we need physical rest when our bodies ache or our immune system is weakened. (*Physical move*: Lay your head on your hands like you are sleeping.)

Mental Rest (16 percent)

When you notice yourself in a brain fog, that is your body communicating it needs mental rest. This means taking a break from the routine through music, meditation, silence, or quiet time alone. (*Physical move*: Tap the sides of your forehead.)

Social Rest (10 percent)

When we feel disconnected from others, it's time to prioritize social time with our friends. (*Physical move*: Open and close your hands like talking mouths.)

Emotional Rest (2 percent)

Feeling underappreciated or misunderstood? If so, you're in need of emotional rest! You would benefit from talking out your troubles with a close friend or professional therapist. This allows someone to help lift your thoughts and spirits during a heavy season. (*Physical move*: Place your hand on your heart.)

Spiritual Rest (2 percent)

This is the feeling of being connected to a higher being or purpose, whether through prayer, reading or listening to devotionals, or giving back to the world through volunteering or community service. Your mind and body will tell you spiritual rest is needed when you feel a lack of purpose or direction. (*Physical move*: Reach out or up with your hands.)

Sensory Rest (2 percent)

Ever find yourself overly agitated and sensitive to sounds or noise? If so, turn off devices, dim the lights, and turn down the noise. (*Physical move*: Say, "Shhh.")

Isn't it interesting that most of the educators we surveyed needed creative, physical, or mental rest? Consider what type(s) of rest you need to feel restored and rejuvenated. Try to create some time and space to honor what your mind, body, and spirit need to feel content, aligned, and balanced.

As Pico Iyer writes in *The Art of Stillness* (2014), "In the age of speed, nothing can be more invigorating than going slow. In an age of distraction, nothing can feel more luxurious than paying attention. In an age of constant movement, nothing is more urgent than sitting still" (p. 66).

TEACH HAPPIER

Small Shifts, Big Gifts

As you move through your week, what two types of rest make you feel most restored? Try and prioritize those types of rest this week. Additionally, consider what type of rest you would like to create more space for, try to do so, and see if it makes a positive impact in your life at work or home. Bonus points if you can also identify the types of rest that restore friends and family members!

Set a personal or professional goal for the week based on one small shift.

Weekly Win: At the end of the week, jot down one great thing that happened.

Objective: Students will learn the seven types of rest and identify the two that are most important to them as well as one that they would like to create more time and space for.

Procedure
1. Read or summarize the chapter for students. For each type of rest, you may wish to use the physical moves provided.
2. Through a think-aloud, share the two types of rest that are most important for you and why.
3. Ask your students to identify which two types of rest are most important in their lives. This is also a natural place for students to discuss *when* they create time for these types of rest.
4. Now think aloud about one type of rest you don't practice often but know would make a positive difference in your life. Explain how you will create time and space to implement this type of rest.
5. Invite students to plan to incorporate one other type of rest. When will they plan to do this?
6. As the weeks progress, continue the conversation by asking students how different types of rest help them feel rejuvenated, grounded, and aligned.

34

Be *Here*

My girlfriends and I have been playing a game for years that we call "Where Are Your Feet?" It's a time to check in with one another and send a picture of our feet that also shows whatever we are doing right at that moment. Sometimes it's lounging on a couch, other times it's sitting on a sideline of our kid's game, still other times it's waiting in line at the store.

Have you ever heard the saying "Be where your feet are"? I've always loved that phrase, because it has the power to shift my thinking to evaluate how present I am at any given moment, whether at school or at home.

So where are *your* feet? This week, I'd like to remind you to be where your feet are, especially at this time of the school year, when things are moving so quickly and so much has to get done.

The notion of "be where your feet are" became clear to me the other day in kickboxing. Allow me to explain.

As part of my ongoing quest to feel rested, energized, and focused, I have enrolled in a 5:30 a.m. Monday morning kickboxing class that helps me begin the week strong. About 15 minutes into class on this particular day, the instructor is preparing us for our next moves, providing modifications as needed. This morning, I'm hanging in there pretty well—but the woman to my left is *killing* it. If our instructor says we can choose to do two burpees or four, this woman does four. Squats? This one is *jump* squatting. Planks? She wants to do plank *jacks*. At 5:45 a.m.

I struggle to breathe and manage my roundhouses, jabs, and hooks, wondering, "How is she doing this? It's cold and dark and early and sweaty and this is hard."

The instructor says to her, "Wow! You are really getting after it today!"

Her response is immediate: "I'm here."

I'm here.

So simple. So profound.

You guys, that's *it*. She was *there*. She made the decision to show up and give it her all.

I realized that I was also there and could also decide to show up—like, *really* show up. So I decided to at least try the extra burpees, jump squats, and plank jacks. Once I did that, the class got a whole lot harder—but it also got a whole lot better. When I left class, I was energized and happy. This shift in my workout also inspired me to think about my upcoming workday and commit to be as present as possible in whatever task I was doing.

As a teacher, where are you during a typical school day? Conducting a small-group reading lesson? Reteaching a math concept that one student just can't get? Moderating a disagreement between two students?

You are *there*. Choose to *really* be there.

Your students are here, right in front of you, for just six more weeks. Are you showing up and giving your all? Because that's what makes us feel connected, energized, and happy. This is such a simple shift, yet profoundly transformational.

When your workday is over, continue to think about where you are. Playing Uno with your children? Keep that phone out of reach. Calling to check in with your aging parents? Find a quiet place so you can really listen and react to what they share. Watching your teenager play soccer? Make sure to watch her closely.

It's a choice you can decide to make about 300 times a day, so do it.

Choose to *show up* and *really be there*.

Small Shifts, Big Gifts

This week, try to be as present as possible both at work and at home. Consider how you can remind yourself to do this—maybe by wearing a certain piece of jewelry, adding something to your ID badge, or setting a phone reminder to help you be as present as possible.

Set a personal or professional goal for the week based on one small shift.

Weekly Win: At the end of the week, jot down one great thing that happened.

35

MYOB

Has anyone ever told you to MYOB—mind your own business? Or have you made this suggestion to others yourself? Here's a little story to illustrate this practice from the perspective of positive psychology.

A colleague of mine confided that a group of teachers at her school were always trying to one-up one another, and it was really getting to her. As we talked, I could tell that her mind and heart were becoming filled with insecurity. This was so disheartening, because she is an *amazing* teacher. "What if it looks like I am not doing all I can?" she asked me. "What if people don't think I'm a good teacher? What if they think I'm lazy?"

What I wanted to say was "Are you kidding me? You are an incredible teacher! How in the world would you ever let anyone get you to question that?!"

But instead, I asked my friend, "Whose business is this?"

"What do you mean?" she said.

"Whose business is this?" I repeated. "Is it *yours? Theirs?* Or does it belong to the *universe?*"

Was it my friend's business that her colleagues were achieving the Pinterest-perfect classroom? Nope. It was *theirs*.

Was it her business they were showing off on Twitter? Nope. That was *their* business.

My friend's shoulders came down and her face softened. "Yes. That's it," she said. "So much of this doesn't have anything to do with me!"

167

Are you waiting for administrators to make the next decision about a district initiative? That's *their* business.

Thinking about the next time a global pandemic will reach our planet? That's the *universe's* business.

Figuring out how to keep you and your family physically and emotionally healthy? *Your* business.

But wondering if that adoption is finally going to go through for your beloved friend? *Universe's* business.

Worried that a colleague feels left out? *Your* business.

But worried that colleague is jealous of something you did or have? *Their* business.

See? Isn't this great? I find this approach so freeing. Don't allow the business of others to take up room in your head or your heart.

Here's to minding your own business.

TEACH HAPPIER

Small Shifts, Big Gifts

Your invitation this week is to sift through and quiet the noise by asking yourself, "Whose business is it—mine, theirs, or the universe's?"

Set a personal or professional goal for the week based on one small shift.

Weekly Win: At the end of the week, jot down one great thing that happened.

Objective: Students will learn how to discern what worries belong to them, others, or the universe by practicing with both classroom-created and real-life scenarios.

Procedure
1. Read or summarize the chapter for students.
2. Create a few scenarios that would be meaningful for your students. Most teachers will take the examples in this chapter and edit them so they're relevant to students.
3. Role-play! Provide students with a scenario and have them talk through how they will identify whether a concern belongs to them, others, or the universe.
4. This strategy works best when it unfolds organically. Keep it in your back pocket to use when students are worrying about social, emotional, or academic events.

36

Minutes and Moments

Think back on the last month. Can you recall one or two beautiful or heartbreaking moments that stood out among the rest? I am sure you can. For me, one such moment would be looking at Niagara Falls with my daughter on a weekend away—or just a few days ago, when I taught a lesson and a student told me the next day how it helped him at home.

A recent heartbreaking moment would be leaving my dad after a few days visiting him in Florida. Although it was a wonderful visit full of sunshine, we're still trying to figure out how to do life without my mom, and the goodbye was sad. As I left to head to the airport, he whispered, "I'm sad to see you go." Though we can usually stay strong for each other, this time we felt too vulnerable not to cry.

These joyful and heartbreaking moments made a difference to my head and heart.

Then there are days like today, that are just normal and routine. Got the kids to school, went to work, had some meetings, scheduled some things, taught a model lesson, emailed a bunch of people, came home to bring my kids where they needed to be, threw in a load of laundry, and made dinner. I feel a little *blah* because none of these events made a difference to my head or heart.

One of my favorite authors is Duke University professor Kate Bowler, who said something recently on a podcast that freed my heart and mind more than anything else has. Kate is one of those rare people in the world, like my mom, who can find beauty and humor tucked in just about anywhere, even when things are challenging. For many of us, this can be hard to do when we feel that things are just . . . normal. Ordinary. Neither forgettable nor memorable. Grocery shopping. Lesson planning. Commuting. Emailing. Meal preparing. Assignment correcting. Faculty meeting-ing.

Here's what's freeing: In episode 57 of Glennon Doyle's (2021c) *We Can Do Hard Things* podcast, Bowler says that it's totally normal to have a beautiful moment or a heartbreaking moment in your day and for that moment to be followed by a bunch of ordinary minutes. In every life, there are minutes and moments—and that's perfectly OK. Not every minute is going to be memorable or life-shifting, and there's nothing wrong with that.

Your invitation this week is to take comfort in the fact that some minutes are just that, and nothing more. Those minutes are the background music for the occasional moments that change our heads and our hearts.

Minutes and moments: It's a both/and situation.

Small Shifts, Big Gifts

TEACH
HAPPIER

What special moments have you experienced at home or at school in the past month or two? How has accepting that there are minutes and moments affected you?

Set a personal or professional goal for the week based on one small shift.

Weekly Win: At the end of the week, jot down one great thing that happened.

37

It's Grow Time

You've heard of post-traumatic stress, but have you heard about what positive psychologists call post-traumatic growth? It's a real thing, and right now I can't stop thinking about it. In a 2019 *Psychology Today* article, Adena Bank Lees defines post-traumatic growth, or PTG, as *"positive psychological change experienced as a result of adversity and other challenges in order to rise to a higher level of functioning"* (para. 1; italics in original).

Adversity? Challenges? Wherever you teach, it's likely you are experiencing both. It may seem hard to admit or overly dramatic, but educators have experienced a level of professional trauma these past few years. There are times when we grieve because our profession has changed so much, or when we can't quiet the noise coming at us from multiple outside groups. We are trying to serve students with profiles that are increasingly challenging. We have more students than ever with individualized needs, student anxiety and depression diagnoses are increasing with students younger than ever before, and there are many outside voices who claim to understand how we can address these needs while we continue to teach, learn, and guide the kids in front of us. We can feel sad, overwhelmed, and brokenhearted.

Recently, I was listening to the podcast *The Next Right Thing* by Emily P. Freeman (2021a). The episode, "Leave It Behind," was about the potential growth we can experience during a time of significant change, and she compared this growth to the growth of a tree. When a seed becomes a sapling and then eventually a tree, it continues growing and changing, but it never goes back to the seed.

It never goes back to the seed.

Reader, this got me. This is totally us right now.

Regardless of where we are in our careers, we can all feel a bit like a brand-new sapling-teacher navigating our current teaching world. Some things that we relied on in the past continue to serve us well, while other things don't.

Return to Adena Bank Lees' definition of post-traumatic growth and look at the last part: *in order to rise to a higher level of functioning.* Colleagues, this is an opportunity for post-traumatic growth. "There are limits that press down on our spirits no matter what fancy mental footwork we're capable of and no matter how much energy we put into it," writes Frank Bruni. "But I do believe we have a say in whether those limits crush and immobilize us" (2022, p. 245).

It's easy to hyperfocus on all that feels wrong and overwhelming. I'm guilty of it some days, too. But when we do that, we are focusing on what we *used* to be—the seed. If we focus instead on how we are growing as teachers and how educational systems and structures are being reevaluated, we can ultimately grow and rise to a higher level of functioning (hello, tree!). Consider having an honest conversation with colleagues about educational equity and access, for example, or reevaluating traditions like back-to-school night or a convoluted rule about how many minutes of homework each grade level should have.

When we are forced to innovate due to traumatic constraints, we should take the opportunity to make improvements that can grow ourselves, our students, and the teaching profession.

Frank Bruni invites us to move from "I can't believe what I'm going through" to "I can't believe what I'm being put through" to "I can't believe what I'm managing to *get* through" (2022, p. 87). Are you here for it?

We can't let our pain go to waste. Let's get growing.

Small Shifts, Big Gifts

Are you able to shift your focus toward the growth that you have experienced over the past few years as an educator? What have you gone through? What have you grown through? Amid all the challenges and frustrations, how have your practices, insights, or skills evolved for the better? How have you experienced growth and wisdom? Set a timer for five minutes and jot down what comes to mind. Recognize and celebrate the tangible growth you have made!

Set a personal or professional goal for the week based on one small shift.

Weekly Win: At the end of the week, jot down one great thing that happened.

38

Choose Your Hard

A few years ago, someone gave me a T-shirt that says, "Choose Happiness." I used to love it, but now it feels a little like toxic positivity. Like, duh, if it were that easy, of course I would simply choose happiness. But it's not that easy.

I recently received an email from a colleague that said, "SUZANNE (yes, I am yelling). This is hard. All of it. I don't even know what to focus on sometimes. Can we talk things through together?" I knew this wasn't a conversation for email, but rather a sit-down chat. I walked in with hot coffee during my colleague's planning period, and I listened as she shared her challenges. *My students need so much more this year than ever before; my own children get the worst version of me because I am so tired; I can't stay on top of grading; I have no energy at this point in the year.*

I sense you nodding your head as you read those italicized words. We could all come up with a similar list of the things in our lives that are hard. Part of the price of admission to life is knowing there are going to be challenges and heartbreak. On her *We Can Do Hard Things* podcast, Glennon Doyle noted that, although happiness can indeed be hard, we get to *choose our hard*. If that doesn't make sense, here are some examples:

- Getting fit is hard. Being unfit is hard. *Choose your hard.*

- Creating new lessons is hard. Teaching the same thing year after year when it may not be exactly right for your students is hard. *Choose your hard.*

- Change is hard. Monotony is hard. *Choose your hard.*

- Nurturing relationships is hard. Not having relationships is hard. *Choose your hard.*

- Learning new strategies to support students with a different profile is hard. Guessing and being unsuccessful is hard. *Choose your hard.*

- Waking up early is hard. Waking up late and rushing is hard. *Choose your hard.*

- Keeping my classroom organized is hard. Constantly trying to find things in a disheveled space is hard. *Choose your hard.*

- Grading papers is hard. Not having data on students is hard. *Choose your hard.*

You see where this is going?

Have you ever heard the saying "The only fair thing about life is that it's unfair to everyone"? While this is true, there are things within your realm of influence and control that you can and should lean into. It's hard, but it's worth it. When making hard decisions, consider which hard thing has the potential to bring you the most amount of happiness, personally or professionally.

I lost one of my best friends, Bev, 10 years ago. She passed away from breast cancer when she was only 36. When she knew that her cancer was terminal, she declared that she was going to "squeeze the heck out of life" for her remaining years. And that's exactly what she did.

Bev loved beautiful things, so she decided to hand-paint an Elise Broach (2008) quote on the sunny yellow bedroom wall that she looked at so often when she became bedridden. We looked at that wall together in her final days as we held hands. The quote Bev painted was "We have so little time, we must spend it as happily as possible."

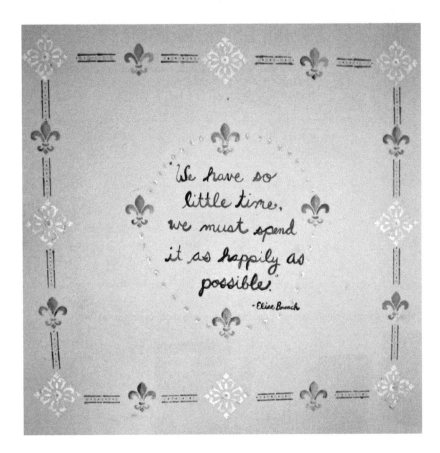

We have so
little time,
we must spend
it as happily as
possible.

- Elise Broach

Go ahead and whisper that last line to yourself: "We have so little time, we must spend it as happily as possible."

What will bring you closer to happiness?

Small Shifts, Big Gifts

How do you anticipate "choose your hard" will show up for you this upcoming week? Can you envision what you will choose?

Set a personal or professional goal for the week based on one small shift.

Weekly Win: At the end of the week, jot down one great thing that happened.

TEACH HAPPIER LESSON

Objective: Students will envision how choosing the right hard can help increase their happiness at school or home.

Procedure

1. Read or summarize the chapter for students.
2. Brainstorm a few "choose your hard" ideas together, like these:

   - Doing homework is hard; not doing homework and feeling unprepared is hard.

   - Keeping your room clean is hard; trying to find things in an unorganized room is hard.

   - Choosing to eat healthy food is hard; eating unhealthy food and feeling tired is hard.

3. Remind students that the choices we are given in our lives are the greatest gifts we have. Allow them time to envision what choices they have in school and at home. They can independently write or type them out and then share with a partner or small group.
4. As a whole class, process some examples of hard choices.
5. As the week progresses, take any natural opportunities to overtly talk about "choosing your hard" (e.g., taking the time to review for an upcoming test, letting someone go ahead of you in the cafeteria or hallway).

39

Summer Stillness

"Oh my gosh, this *year!*" is a common phrase as summer break approaches. During the summer, you'll need to prioritize rest and rejuvenation as much as you can so that, when it's time to return in the fall, you can face it with grace and perspective. Consider how much it might help if you allowed yourself to become still throughout the summer. What would it do for your mind, body, and spirit?

Think about an ocean with choppy water: The water is moving so fast that you can't see through it. Now think about an ocean with still water: You can see right through it; everything is clear. Stillness brings clarity. Pico Iyer (2014), author of *The Art of Stillness*, reminds us, "Going nowhere isn't about turning your back on the world; it's about stepping away now and then so you can see the world more clearly and love it more deeply" (p. 13).

If we allow ourselves to be still, we can squeeze the heck out of every unrushed, unplugged, serene summer moment by creating space for *intentional* time away. Free time doesn't always mean availability. We must remember that balance isn't found; it's created. We have to get disciplined with how we can make this a part of our summer days.

Even if you have family responsibilities that make stillness a challenge, it is still attainable! Start with just 30 minutes. I create sustained stillness twice a day, once in the morning and once in the evening. On these warmer days, I am certain that my 15 minutes on the porch with coffee before anyone wakes up and my 15 minutes reading a book at the end of the day create stillness and provide an opportunity to align my heart and my mind. This daily practice has made a significant positive impact on my overall emotional wellness, and it could do the same for you.

Next fall is going to be a hustle no matter what. It always takes unwavering energy, enthusiasm, and optimism to get our schools, classrooms, and materials ready for students to return. The only way you'll generate these feelings is by conserving and creating energy by prioritizing stillness this summer.

Take a deep breath. Get still.

Small Shifts, Big Gifts

How will you encourage stillness this summer?

Set a personal or professional goal for the week based on one small shift.

Weekly Win: At the end of the week, jot down one great thing that happened.

40

Be Like Beverly

If you flip back to the beginning of this book, you will see that I dedicated it to two of my favorite teachers: my beloved mom, Beverly Elaine, and my beautiful daughter, Emerson Elaine. If you remember one story from this entire book, I want it to be this one. I wrote it nine months before my mom passed away. It's an invitation to be more like Beverly.

Beverly was my angel here on Earth for over 40 years. Her unconditional love sustained, strengthened, and protected me. The greatest honor of my life is being her daughter. She is the most loving, kindhearted, generous, and genuine person I have ever known.

Growing up in a tiny town in western New York, we lived a very modest life in a drafty old farmhouse and held gratitude up as *the* most important family value. At dinner, instead of asking, "How was your day?" my mom would ask questions like, "Who helped you today? Who did you help? When did you laugh the hardest?" Without my brother or I ever knowing it, throughout our childhood we were being conditioned to consistently scan for the good stuff as we looked at life through the lens of abundance and gratitude.

As our relationship evolved through the years, conversations between my mom and me always came naturally. We saw the world similarly, giggled a lot, and could always tell what the other person was thinking with a quick look. Toward the end of her life, as Alzheimer's took its toll, carrying on a conversation became different, requiring careful thought on my part to ensure my mom could engage confidently.

Shortly before my mom was unable to leave the house for safety reasons, I took her to the grocery store. As we were getting out of the car, I realized she didn't have her mask, so I gently reminded her: "Mom, don't forget your mask—I know I do all the time." As she slowly looped the elastic around her ears, she said, "Aren't these just the best things? They are so comfortable!" I smiled and thought, only my mom would call the masks we all had to wear during the COVID-19 pandemic "the best."

Then, as we were walking into the store, she said, "You know what's crazy? We are going to walk in here and they are going to have everything we need! How great is that?!" The tears reached my eyes before my heart managed to capture the beauty of her words.

The mask. The store. She saw beauty in it all. She couldn't *not* see beauty in it all.

If it was sunny, she'd say the sky looked beautiful; on a rainy day, she'd explain how good it was for the trees and the flowers. On a still day, she'd describe how the pine trees in her yard majestically stood against the sky; if it was a windy day, she'd say it felt refreshing. And anytime she saw a sunset, she'd declare, often with tears in her eyes, that it was the most beautiful thing she'd ever seen.

In her final weeks, my mom could hardly form coherent sentences. But she always said thank you, closed her eyes to savor a sip of cold water, hugged every nurse who walked through the door, and would muster up every ounce of energy to convey to her family and friends that she loved them through her sweet voice and beautiful blue eyes.

Do you see it? At the end of her life, my mom, who had lived the last 67 years anchored in profound gratitude and abundance, *could now only scan for the good.* As Alzheimer's took hold and her mental capacity weakened, she hung on to the good stuff. The abundance. The blessings. These were the things she could embrace at this stage of the disease.

How beautiful is that?

Will I one day suffer from Alzheimer's? Unfortunately, research tells me it's likely. But if I can use Mom's example to live a life grounded in gratitude and abundance *now* and continue to scan for good, I'll still be doing so at the very end.

I cannot imagine a lesson more important than this. This is why my mom will forever be my favorite teacher.

As your yearlong journey comes to an end, your invitation moving forward is to be a little more like Beverly Elaine Olney.

Remember gratitude. Remember love.

There's no greater legacy to leave.

TEACH
HAPPIER

Small Shifts, Big Gifts

Is there anyone in your life who reminds you of Beverly? Someone who naturally scans for the good and expresses gratitude for everything? Celebrate that person and consider how you can be more like them to live a life grounded in abundance and gratitude.

Set a personal or professional goal for the week based on one small shift.

Weekly Win: At the end of the week, jot down one great thing that happened.

Objective: Students will share what resonated with them to create a goal for school or home.

Procedure

1. Read or summarize the chapter for students.
2. Give students three to four minutes to independently write or type what resonated with them from this story about Beverly.
3. Have students share thoughts with partners or small groups.
4. Facilitate a whole-group conversation in which you encourage students to consider a goal for school or home.
5. Model a goal of your own (e.g., I will try to ask my children deeper questions at dinnertime; I will try to find at least one thing a day that I find beautiful).
6. Allow students two to three minutes to create their goals. Offer them the opportunity to share with the class if time allows.

CARD

4

To achieve happiness I advocate four major principles:
love, wisdom, self-reflection, and progress.

— Rhuho Okawa —

You did it! You made it through another school year! As you now wind down and enter those delicious early days of summer, take a moment to reflect as you have throughout the year, and direct your next small shifts in thoughts, language, and actions.

TAKEAWAYS

Review and summarize what was meaningful to you during the last 10 weeks.

31. The Fourth Quarter Is Yours
32. Extreme Phone Makeover
33. Rest Happier
34. Be *Here*
35. MYOB
36. Minutes and Moments
37. It's Grow Time
38. Choose Your Hard
39. Summer Stillness
40. Be Like Beverly

Reflections

Scan for the good! Review your Weekly Wins. What is something that makes you proud or especially happy? Are these Weekly Wins helping you tell the story you recorded in the "Before You Begin" chapter on page 7?

Name one or two small shifts you've incorporated in your personal or professional life that have made a positive impact at work and/ or at home. These may be shifts you want to incorporate long term. Can you articulate the impact of these small shifts in your life?

Name one or two small shifts you didn't have the bandwidth for earlier but want to practice soon. What do you hope to accomplish by incorporating these small shifts in your personal or professional life?

Look back to your original happiness baseline (see Figure i.1 on p. 6). Overall, are you feeling more content and aligned now? If so, describe how. If not, consider what small shifts in thoughts, language, or actions could help you feel an increase in your overall happiness at work or at home.

Where would you place yourself on the happiness continuum today? If possible, jot down a few reasons why.

Conclusion:
Ending the School Year

Well, here you are at the very end of another school year. No doubt you are tired, a bit relieved, and ready for some well-deserved rest. Hopefully you will continue to learn from your past as you look to your future.

Remember this? It's the pledge I suggested you strive for at the beginning of the year:

> As a rational optimist, I will know what I can incorporate in my personal and professional life to feel as content, aligned, and balanced as realistically possible.

When you began this journey at the start of the school year, you did some deep reflection and set some goals for yourself. Now that you're rounding out this year as an educator, reflect on your goals and celebrate the growth you've experienced.

Life at Home and School

Add your reflections to Reflection Boxes A and B.

Reflection Box A

What Worked (Professionally)	What Didn't Work (Professionally)

What Worked (Personally)	What Didn't Work (Personally)

Reflection Box B

What Was Life GIVING? (Professionally)	What Was Life DRAINING? (Professionally)
What Was Life GIVING? (Personally)	**What Was Life DRAINING? (Personally)**
What Is Something Positive I Want to Acknowledge or Remember?	**What Is Something Negative I Want to Acknowledge or Remember?**

Look back at what you wrote in Reflection Box 3 (p. 5) at the beginning of the school year. How do your goals compare with the reality? Reflect here using Reflection Box C.

Reflection Box C

Beginning of the Year	End of the Year	General Reflections
How did YOU want to feel at the end of the year?	How do YOU feel?	
How did you want your STUDENTS to feel at the end of the year?	How do your STUDENTS feel?	
How did you want your COLLEAGUES to feel at the end of the year?	How do your COLLEAGUES feel?	
How did you want your FAMILY to feel at the end of the year?	How does your FAMILY feel?	

Relationships

Use Reflection Box D to reflect on the relationships you've nurtured over the past year.

Reflection Box D

Relationships I've Nurtured in the Past Year	Impact on My Overall Happiness

Your Happiness Baseline

Now reflect again on the happiness continuum, shown in Figure i.1 (p. 6). Where do you fall on this scale now? Take the space that follows to write down a few reasons *why* you feel the way you feel now.

Your Story

Think back on the "Before You Begin" chapter near the beginning of this book and the story you wanted to tell this year. What story did you end up telling? Use Reflection Box E to reflect on your story.

Reflection Box E

The Story I *Wanted* to Tell This Year	The Story I *Did* Tell This Year	General Thoughts/ Reflections

Final Thought

Now reflect on the essential question presented at the start of this book: What practices based in positive psychology will make a positive impact in my life, personally and professionally?

Objective: Students will summarize their takeaways from the Teach Happier lessons.

Procedure
1. To activate prior learning, remind students of the lesson titles you shared with them by displaying them on the board.
2. Allow students 5–10 minutes to talk with a partner (or, ideally, a small group) to process some takeaways. You can use guiding questions like these:

    *   What do you remember from these lessons?

    *   What have you tried at school or at home that has made a positive impact?

    *   Did these lessons seem to help your overall feeling of happiness? Why or why not?

    *   Try to summarize this learning in one or two sentences.

Acknowledgments

To my cherished home team, Pat, Emerson, and Ryan. You have the magical way of making me feel held and free at the same time, and I'll never get over the fact that you are mine. Thank you for your encouragement as I worked to make this dream come true. My favorite thing in the whole wide world is making dreams come true together. I am so darn proud of us and the life we've built here in our own little corner of the world in beautiful Doylestown. (Pat, if you are still reading these words, I am so proud of you for reading all the pages of a book! Yay, you!)

To my original home team, my beloved parents. Thank you for being my first teachers. Having you as parents has been an embarrassment of riches and the honor of my lifetime. You've loved me through everything and always made me feel safe, seen, and supported. Dad, thank you for cheering me on each and every day here on Earth as Mom echoes those cheers from Heaven. And Mom, look! You're still teaching! I am so grateful some of your life lessons can carry on in this book. You are still changing this world with your legacy of love.

To my western New York team, my hometown family. Brian, they say a happy childhood lasts forever. I'm so grateful for the childhood we shared on Priem Road and the family memories we continue to make together. Thank you for always getting the band together to eat, drink, and be merry, and obvi, thank you for giving me such a fun sister-in-law and two of the best nieces an auntie could ask for. Frank and Marianne, can a daughter-in-law get any luckier?! Thank you for loving me like your own for over 25 years now. I love you so much and cherish the time and laughs we share. Talamora Daileys, I *love* the memories we make together and count the days until our next family shenanigans. GO BILLS!

To my Olney/King team: Thank you for the love and encouragement you have given me over four decades and for believing in this dream. Our memories together are some of the best ones, and it's not lost on me that not everyone gets an extended family that's such a good time! Nan, you are not only a hot ticket, but also the best matriarch a family could ask for. You have taught me that a good life is one filled with family, laughter, and delicious homemade pizza. Thank you for displaying my poems when I was little—you always made me feel like a real writer. Liz and Jackie, I promise to keep calling you at every DPC. We want to be just like you when we grow up.

To the team of my heart, my net of girlfriends. Whether close by in Pennsylvania or in another state, you have loved me like a sister for as long as I can remember, through the best and worst times of my life. Your steadfast love has sustained me more times than I could ever count. Our laughter, memories, and time together are some of the most beautiful gifts I'll ever receive. I'm so thankful we get to do life together.

To my work team, my CB family. My goodness, it doesn't get better than you. My imagination won't allow me to fathom working alongside anyone other than you. Thank you for believing in me and allowing me to stretch my wings at something new. I felt your unwavering support with every word I wrote. You are such an important part of my home here in Pennsylvania.

And how could I not mention my teacher team? The teachers who've loved, challenged, guided, and supported me. I carry your lessons to students every day. From Brockport Central School District: my 1st grade teacher, Mrs. Howland, who helped me fall in love with writing; my 2nd grade teacher, Mrs. Fesseden, who typed my words and made me feel like a real author; and Mrs. Nelson, my 4th grade teacher, who made me dream of having my own classroom of 4th graders one day. From Niagara University: Dr. Pollard and Dr.

Martin—you both opened my eyes and heart to texts that changed me forever. I've never worked harder in classes than I did in yours, and I am so grateful you pushed me.

To my small but mighty spiritual team, Pastors Thomas Rusert and Dr. Robert Linders: Not only are you my favorite pastors, you're also two of my favorite teachers. You give me things to think about that make me better at home and at school. Thank you for inviting me to find visible signs of invisible grace wherever I go.

To my PLN team: Rob Dunlop, I could have never gotten through this journey without you. Thank you for helping me navigate my first rodeo and making me believe every step of the way that I could do this. To Rae and Jeff from Teach Better, thank you for opening doors for me to share this work. And look, Adam Welcome! The podcast became a thing! Thank you for holding me accountable and helping this book become a reality. Lauren, thank you for turning some of these ideas into lessons for kids. I am honored you share them with your students, and co-teaching with you has been life-giving.

To my team of angels, Bev, Corinne, and Mindy. Thank you for sharing a part of your life with me; you have a permanent place in my heart. Your presence is felt every day, and you are so, so missed. The lessons you've taught me inspired the reflections in this book. Your beautiful lives prove that our broken hearts can still burst with love and gratitude.

Last but not least, to my grassroots Teach Happier team: Thank you for growing this wonderful community. I love the energy we share with one another. I appreciate you letting me share some ideas from the floor of my unorganized closet so we can spend a few minutes together each week.

And thank you, dear readers, for sharing your time with the words in this book. I sincerely hope it has helped your head and heart. You've helped make a lifelong dream come true.

Appendix:
Collegial Conversations

Are you ready to talk about your learning with colleagues, or looking for low-prep ways for your faculty or team to share key takeaways? The following are a few ideas to help organize these collegial conversations.

Turn and Learn (5–10 minutes)
Reserve 5–10 minutes once a month at faculty, department, or leadership meetings to engage in a Turn and Learn. Choose from the following prompts to scaffold the conversation (try choosing one per meeting):

- At this point in the book, what are your key takeaways?
- What strategies have you implemented that have benefited you at work or at home?
- What strategies or lessons have you shared with students? Describe their impact.
- What have you read that affirms your thinking? What have you read that challenges your thinking?
- Review your latest "Report Card" reflection and share something with the group that you think could give colleagues insight or something to consider.

As educators share their responses, allow time for colleagues to ask questions to dig deeper into the application of the strategies and their takeaways.

Tech option! This exercise can easily be done within your network using discussion boards, a backchannel, or programs like FlipGrid or Padlet. You can do this in real time or keep it open so colleagues can add to it continually.

3 in 3 (5 minutes)

- Set a timer for three minutes. Educators will write down as many three-word phrases as they can to summarize their key learning/takeaways (examples: work/life satisfaction, goal for bedtime, just say no, mind my business, be like Beverly). It's OK if the phrases aren't grammatically perfect. The goal is to get to the heart of their takeaways!
- At the end of the three minutes, ask each person to circle their favorite phrase. Depending on the size of your group, share in small- or whole-group reflection.

Tech option! Colleagues can share their favorite 3 in 3 using programs like Mentimeter, Padlet, or any interactive whiteboard or notebook that comes with your software suite.

Carousel Walk (10 minutes)

- Label three pieces of chart paper with one of the following headings at the top: small shifts in THOUGHTS, small shifts in LANGUAGE, and small shifts in ACTIONS. Hang the chart paper around the room.
- Set a timer for five minutes.
- Have educators walk around and add their takeaways to the charts until the timer goes off. Some like to ask folks to add their initials to their notes, and some prefer to leave them anonymous. Choose whatever would work best for your group.
- Now set a timer for three minutes and have colleagues walk around to each paper and annotate the notes with one of the following symbols:

    ★ "I agree!"

    ! "We need to remember this as a group!"

    ? "I have a question about this."

- For the final two minutes, the facilitator can help summarize individual and collective thoughts and takeaways to anchor future discussions or investigations.

Note: If working with a large group, you may need to create duplicates of the three chart papers to accommodate your group within the 10-minute period.

Tech option! This activity could be accomplished using Google Jamboard or any interactive whiteboard or notebook that comes with your software suite.

Bibliography

Achor, S. (2010). *The happiness advantage: How a positive brain fuels success in work and life*. Crown.

Achor, S. (2018). *Big potential: How transforming the pursuit of success raises our achievement, happiness, and well-being*. Penguin Random House.

Achor, S. (2021, November 23). There's a reason your free time is so draining [Blog post]. *Success*. https://www.success.com/why-your-free-time-is-so-draining/

Aguilar, E. (2021, December 5). How year-end reflection fosters resilience. *Educational Leadership*, 79(4). https://www.ascd.org/el/articles/the-resilient-educator-how-year-end-reflection-fosters-resilience

Baltazzi, M. (2018). Why science says helping others makes us happier. *Thrive*. https://thriveglobal.com/stories/why-science-says-helping-others-makes-us-happier/

Bank Lees, A. (2019, April 18). Posttraumatic growth: There can be positive change after adversity [Blog post]. *Psychology Today*. https://www.psychologytoday.com/us/blog/surviving-thriving/201904/posttraumatic-growth

Beck, M. (2002). Do you need more fun in your life? *Oprah.com*. https://www.oprah.com/spirit/why-you-need-more-fun-in-your-life-martha-beck/all

Borresen, K. (2020, May 21). The psychological benefits of having things to look forward to. *HuffPost*. https://www.huffpost.com/entry/psychological-benefits-things-look-forward-to_l_5ec40575c5b62696fb60e3a1

Broach, E. (2008). *Masterpiece*. Henry Holt.

Brooks, G. (2021, January). *Climate and culture in schools*. Keynote address delivered at the ASCD Virtual Conference.

Brown, B. (2015). *Rising strong: The reckoning. The rumble. The revolution*. Random House.

Brown, B. (2017). *Braving the wilderness: The quest for true belonging and the courage to stand alone*. Random House.

Brown, B. (2018). *Dare to lead: Brave work. Tough conversations. Whole hearts*. Random House.

Brown, B. (2021a). *Atlas of the heart: Mapping meaningful connection and the language of human experience*. Random House.

Brown, B. (2021b, February 24). Recognizing the choices and gifts in our lives [Podcast episode]. *Unlocking Us*. https://brenebrown.com /podcast/brene-with-dr-edith-eger-on-recognizing-the-choices-and-gifts-in-our-lives/

Bruni, F. (2022). *The beauty of dusk: On vision lost and found*. Simon & Schuster.

Casas, J. (2019, February). *Live your excellence*. Keynote address, Central Bucks School District, Doylestown, Pennsylvania.

Cedars-Sinai staff. (2019, February 13). The science of kindness [Blog post]. *Cedars-Sinai*. https://www.cedars-sinai.org/blog/science-of-kindness.html

Chowdhury, M. R. (2019, April 9). The neuroscience of gratitude and how it affects anxiety and grief. *PositivePsychology.com*. https://positive psychology.com/neuroscience-of-gratitude

Clark, B. (2019). Why rational optimism is the key to success and less stress. *Further*. https://further.net/rational-optimism/

Clear, J. (2018). *Atomic habits: An easy and proven way to build good habits and break bad ones*. Penguin Random House.

Clear, J. (2019). 3-2-1: On comparison, consistency, and what's not going to change. *The 3-2-1 Newsletter*. https://jamesclear.com/3-2-1/september-19-2019

Corrigan, K. (2021). Mental health check on the "most important" thing [Podcast episode]. *Kelly Corrigan Wonders*. PRX. https://beta.prx.org/stories/399062

Couros, G. (2018, February). *The innovator's mindset*. Keynote address, Central Bucks School District, Doylestown, PA.

Covey, S. (2004). *7 habits of highly effective people: Powerful lessons in personal change*. Simon & Schuster.

Dalton-Smith, S. (2017). *Sacred rest: Recover your life, renew your energy, reclaim your life*. FaithWords.

Dalton-Smith, S. (2021, January 6). The 7 types of rest that every person needs [Blog post]. *TED*. https://ideas.ted.com/the-7-types-of-rest-that-every-person-needs

David, S. (2016). *Emotional agility: Get unstuck, embrace change, and thrive in work and life*. Penguin.

Doyle, G. (2014, January 30). Share this with all the schools, please [Blog post]. *We Can Do Hard Things*. https://momastery.com/blog/2014/01/30/share-schools/

Doyle, G. (2018, March). We can do hard things. Speech, Pennridge Middle School, Pennridge, PA.

Doyle, G. (2021a, October 21). Creativity, chemistry, & claiming your joy [Podcast episode]. *We Can Do Hard Things*. https://momastery.com/blog/we-can-do-hard-things-ep-37

Doyle, G. (2021b, November 4). Landing in love: Is the settling-in phase the best stage of love? [Podcast episode]. *We Can Do Hard Things*. https://momastery.com/blog/we-can-do-hard-things-ep-41

Doyle, G. (2021c, December 30). Walking our people through hard things [Podcast episode]. *We Can Do Hard Things.* https://momastery.com/blog/we-can-do-hard-things-ep-57

Doyle, G. (2022, January 13). Are your friendships draining or charging you? [Podcast episode]. *We Can Do Hard Things.* https://momastery.com/blog/we-can-do-hard-things-ep-61

Dunlop, R. (2020). *STRIVE for happiness in education.* EduMatch.

Economist, The. (2010, December 16). Age and happiness: The U-bend of life. https://docs.google.com/file/d/0BxzNKuWVerMWeHNpYVZjVFh3Z3M

Feeney, B. C., & Collins, N. L. (2014). A new look at social support: A theoretical perspective on thriving through relationships. *Personality and Social Psychology Review, 19*(2), 113–147.

Frankl, V. E. (2006). *Man's search for meaning.* Beacon Press.

Freeman, E. (2019). *The next right thing.* Revell Publishers.

Freeman, E. (2021a, May). Leave it behind [Podcast episode]. *The Next Right Thing.* https://emilypfreeman.com/podcast/138/

Freeman, E. (2021b). *The next right thing guided journal: A decision-making companion.* Revell Publishers.

Goff, B. (2022). *Undistracted: Capture your purpose, rediscover your joy.* Nelson Books.

Hattie, J. (2012). *Visible learning for teachers: Maximizing impact on learning.* Routledge.

Hurd, S. (2014). New study reveals the link between strong relationships and success. www.learning-mind.com/new-study-reveals-the-link-between-strong-relationships-and-success/

Iyer, P. (2014). *Art of stillness: Adventures in going nowhere.* Simon & Schuster.

Koester, M. (2018, January 17). An exploration of mood tracking: Can we measure how we feel? [Blog post]. *Mark Koester.* www.markwk.com/2018/01/limits-to-mood-tracking.html

Krasinski, J. (2020). *Some Good News.* https://www.youtube.com/c/SomeGoodNews

Merlin, S. (2018, May). Can you make yourself more lucky? *Merlin Works.* https://www.merlin-works.com/2018/06/19/can-you-make-yourself-more-lucky-merlin-works-may-2018-newsletter/

Nortje, A. (2020, April 29). Social comparison theory & 12 real-life examples. *PositivePsychology.com.* https://positivepsychology.com/social-comparison/

Peck, M. (2012). *The road less traveled: A new psychology on love, traditional values, and spiritual growth.* Simon & Schuster.

Psychology Today staff. (2022). Happiness over the lifespan. *Psychology Today.* https://www.psychologytoday.com/us/basics/happiness/happiness-over-the-lifespan

Rubin, G. (2007, August 30). A key to happiness: Having something to look forward to. *Gretchen Rubin.* https://gretchenrubin.com/2007/08/a-key-to-happ-2/

Rubin, G. (2009a). *The happiness project: Or, why I spent a year trying to sing in the morning, clean my closets, fight right, read Aristotle, and generally have more fun.* HarperCollins.

Rubin, G. (2009b). *The happiness project one-sentence journal.* HarperCollins.

Rubin, G. (2015). *Better than before: What I learned about making and breaking habits—To sleep more, quit sugar, procrastinate less, and generally build a happier life.* Crown.

Rubin, G. (2020). *Outer order, inner calm: Declutter and organize to make more room for happiness.* Two Roads.

Schnall, S., Harber, K. D., Stefanucci, J. K., & Proffitt, D. R. (2008). Social support and the perception of geographical slant. *Journal of Experimental Social Psychology, 44*(5), 1246–1255.

Siegle, S. (2020, May 29). The art of kindness. *Mayo Clinic Health System.* https://www.mayoclinichealthsystem.org/hometown-health/speaking-of-health/the-art-of-kindness

Stickgold, R., Malia, A., Maguire, D., Roddenberry, D., & O'Connor, M. (2020). Replaying the game: Hypnagogic images in normals and amnesics. *Science, 290*(5490), 350–353.

Tawwab, N. (2021). *Set boundaries, find peace: A guide to reclaiming yourself.* Penguin Random House.

Thetford, S. (2018, October 12). The difference between "work-life balance" and "work-life satisfaction." *Sendero.* www.senderoconsulting.com/work-life-satisfaction/

Titova, L., & Sheldon, K. M. (2021). Happiness comes from trying to make others feel good, rather than oneself. *The Journal of Positive Psychology, 17*(3), 341–355.

Tracy, B. (2017). *Eat that frog! 21 ways to stop procrastinating and get more done in less time.* Barrett-Koehler Publishers.

Travers, M. (2021, May 27). Happiness comes from making others feel good [Blog post]. *Psychology Today.* https://www.psychologytoday.com/us/blog/social-instincts/202105/happiness-comes-making-others-feel-good

Volpe, A. (2020, December 29). Science says you need to plan some things to look forward to. *Vice.* www.vice.com/amp/en/article/7k9wvb/science-says-you-need-future-plans-to-look-forward-to-during-pandemic

Wambach, A. (2019). *Wolfpack: How to come together, unleash our power, and change the game.* Celadon Books.

White, K. (2017, December 28). Working with the overwhelmed nervous system. *Belvedere Integrated Healing Arts.* http://www.belvederearts.com/eye-of-the-needle-near-death-experience/working-with-the-overwhelmed-nervous-system

Winfrey, O. (2017, September 17). Don Miguel Ruiz: Find freedom, happiness and love [Podcast episode]. *Oprah's Super Soul Conversations.* OWN. https://super-soul.simplecast.com/episodes/don-miguel-ruiz-find-freedom-happiness-and-love

Wiseman, R. (2003). The luck factor. *The Skeptical Inquirer, 27,* 1–5.

Wong, B. (2021, April 5). What is toxic productivity? Here's how to spot the damaging behavior. *HuffPost.* www.huffpost.com/entry/toxic-productivity-work_l_606655e7c5b6aa24bc60a566

Zucker, R. (2019, October 10). How to deal with constantly feeling overwhelmed. *Harvard Business Review.* https://hbr.org/2019/10/how-to-deal-with-constantly-feeling-overwhelmed

Index

About the Author

 **Suzanne Dailey** has been an educator for 20 years and is an instructional coach in the Central Bucks School District, the third-largest school district in Pennsylvania. There she has the honor and joy of working with over 600 elementary teachers and 9,000 students. She teaches model lessons, facilitates professional development sessions, and mentors teachers to be the best they can be for the students in front of them.

Suzanne holds National Board Certification and is a fellow of the National Writing Project. She has a master's degree in reading. She is dedicated to nurturing and developing the whole child and teacher and presents these topics both in person and virtually at the local, state, and national levels (see her website, www.suzannedailey.com, for testimonials). Suzanne also presents sessions to corporations outside the education field on such topics as positive psychology, motivation, and leadership.

Suzanne is the host of the weekly podcast *Teach Happier*. This five-minute podcast is enjoyed by listeners around the world, and the community is growing each day. In addition to this podcast, Suzanne writes a monthly blog for the Teach Better team at www.teachbetter.com/tag/teach-happier-series.

Suzanne lives in Doylestown, Pennsylvania, with her husband, two children, and English bulldog. You can follow her on Twitter at @DaileySuzanne, subscribe to the *Teach Happier* podcast, and join the Teach Happier community at www.suzannedailey.com.

Related ASCD Resources

At the time of publication, the following resources were available (ASCD stock numbers appear in parentheses).

Print Products

The Burnout Cure: Learning to Love Teaching Again by Chase Mielke (#119004)

Committing to the Culture: How Leaders Can Create and Sustain Positive Schools by Steve Gruenert and Todd Whitaker (#119007)

Compassionate Coaching: How to Help Educators Navigate Barriers to Professional Growth by Kathy Perret and Kenny McKee (#121017)

Educator Bandwidth: How to Reclaim Your Energy, Passion, and Time by Jane Kise and Ann Holm (#122019)

Leadership for Learning: How to Bring Out the Best in Every Teacher, 2nd Edition by Carl Glickman and Rebecca West Burns (#121007)

Mindfulness in the Classroom: Strategies for Promoting Concentration, Compassion, and Calm by Thomas Armstrong (#120018)

Overcoming Educator Burnout (Quick Reference Guide) by Chase Mielke (#QRG123016)

The Principal as Chief Empathy Officer: Creating a Culture Where Everyone Grows by Thomas R. Hoerr (#122030)

Stress-Busting Strategies for Teachers: How do I manage the pressures of teaching? (ASCD Arias) by M. Nora Mazzone and Barbara J. Miglionico (#SF114071)

Teaching with Empathy: How to Transform Your Practice by Understanding Your Learners by Lisa Westman (#121027)

The Well-Balanced Teacher: How to Work Smarter and Stay Sane Inside the Classroom and Out by Mike Anderson (#111004)

Well-Being in Schools: Three Forces That Will Uplift Your Students in a Volatile World by Andy Hargreaves and Dennis Shirley (#122025)

For up-to-date information about ASCD resources, go to www.ascd. org. You can search the complete archives of *Educational Leadership* at www.ascd.org/el.

ASCD myTeachSource®

Download resources from a professional learning platform with hundreds of research-based best practices and tools for your classroom at http://myteachsource.ascd.org/.

For more information, send an email to member@ascd.org; call 1-800-933-2723 or 703-578-9600; send a fax to 703-575-5400; or write to Information Services, ASCD, 2800 Shirlington Road, Suite 1001, Arlington, VA 22206 USA.